ANSWER BOOK

to accompany

The Little, Brown Workbook

ANSWER BOOK

to accompany

The Little, Brown Workbook

EIGHTH EDITION

Prepared by

Donna Gorrell
St. Cloud State University

Longman

New York Boston San Francisco
London Toronto Sydney Tokyo Singapore Madrid
Mexico City Munich Paris Cape Town Hong Kong Montreal

Answer Book to accompany *The Little, Brown Handbook,* Eighth Edition

Please visit our Web site at *http://www.awl.com/littlebrown*.

ISBN: 0-321-08787-9

2 3 4 5 6 7 8 9 10- VG -03 02 01

TO THE STUDENT: USING THE ANSWER KEY

This key is intended to help you work though the exercises in *The Little, Brown Workbook*, Eighth Edition. With it, you can check your answers to the exercises as soon as you have completed them, while the problems they presented and the thinking you applied to those problems are still fresh in your mind. We suggest you use the answer key in the following way.

Always try to complete an entire exercise before consulting the answers. If an item gives you trouble, refer to the text of the workbook—or to *The Little, Brown Handbook,* Eighth Edition, if it is assigned—for a rule or example that pertains to the problem. Consult the answers only after you have completed the entire exercise. Resolve any differences between your answers and the ones given here by referring again to the text. If the reason for the differences does not become clear, ask your instructor for an explanation.

The answers labeled *Sample answers* are provided as examples for exercises that do not have a single right answer. Your response—based on your own background and your own judgments about how to revise a sentence or a paragraph—may be quite different and still be correct. Because of differences of opinion about what constitutes appropriate usage, the same may be true even of some exercises for which one "right" answer is given. Thus you and your instructor may disagree with an answer shown here, not necessarily because it is wrong but because it represents only one interpretation.

CONTENTS

I THE WRITING PROCESS

CHAPTER 1

Assessing Your Writing Situation

Exercise 1-1, p. 7. Discovering a subject

No sample answers.

Exercise 1-2, p. 9 Analyzing Audience and Purpose

No sample answers.

Exercise 1-3, p. 11. Analyzing tone and purpose

Sample answers:

1. The tone is complaining, critical, perhaps hostile. The writer "bristled" and "cursed" his hair. He was "infuriated" by the "taunting" and the "pandering." He probably wants the audience to be sympathetic to a boy's desire to be heroic like Johnny Quest.
2. The tone is critical but humorous, rather conversational. Gray is intent on entertaining his audience.
3. The paragraph appears to be satirical—of both baby boomers and the churches that adapt to their varied expectations. The comparison of the modern church to "that other late- century cathedral, the mall" exemplifies the satire. Trueheart evidently wants the audience to enjoy the fun, though some students may be put off by the criticism of the church.

CHAPTER 2

Developing and Shaping Your Ideas

Exercise 2-1, p. 25. Developing a subject through freewriting

No sample answers.

Exercise 2-2, p. 25. Generating ideas

No sample answers.

Exercise 2-3, p. 26. Thesis Statement: Revising

Sample answers:

1. Because most professional athletes get six-figure salaries and have many fringe benefits such as a four-month winter vacation, many people believe they have no right to strike.
2. At a time when life has become dominated by technology and science and when organized religion has become as bureaucratic as big business, many people turn to religious cults as a source of meaning and value.
3. If government is responsible for ensuring life, liberty, and the pursuit of happiness for all citizens, a guaranteed college education should be a legitimate part of that responsibility.
4. Because some wild animals become so numerous that their environment no longer can provide enough food for them, hunting them may actually help maintain the balance of nature.
5. Travel to foreign countries has increased my knowledge, enriched me with new experiences, and taught me how other people live.
6. Remaining silent rather than expressing anger often prevents me from saying something I would later regret.

Exercise 2-4, p. 27. Thesis Statement: Developing

No sample answers.

Exercise 2-5, p. 28. The formal outline

Sample answer:

I. Introduction
  A. Narrative of last plane trip
  B. Recounting fear of flying
  C. Statement of thesis
II. Relaxation methods before a flight
  A. Trying to sleep the night before
    1. Reading an architecture book before sleeping
    2. Contemplating pictures before sleeping
  B. Riding to the airport
    1. Talking to the cab driver
    2. Looking out the cab window
  C. Reading in the airport lounge
III. Relaxation methods during a flight
  A. Taking a seat
    1. Choosing a location
    2. Choosing a travel companion
  B. Eating
  C. Reading
  D. Listening to music
  E. Staying in my seat
  F. Refraining from looking out the window
IV. Conclusion and restatement of thesis

Exercise 2-6, p. 29. Outlining an essay

Sample answer:

Thesis: It wasn't easy adjusting from Spanish to English when everyone around me was speaking English.

I. Introduction
  A. Setting the scene as a Spanish speaker
  B. Establishing the difficulty of becoming adept at a second language
II. Background
  A. Learning English in school while growing up in Mexico
  B. Watching English-language television and reading English-language newspapers
  C. Frustrations of not understanding
III. Move to United States
  A. Difficulty of English-language immersion
  B. Student guides, study buddies, and tutors
IV. Adjusting outside of school
  A. Teasing because of accent
  B. Advice from mother
V. Conclusion—adjustment to English as dominant language

Exercise 2-7, p. 31. Writing an outline for an essay

No sample answer.

CHAPTER 3

Drafting and Revising

Exercise 3-1, p. 45. Revising the first draft

Sample answer:

I think you have a good idea in explaining the importance of sociology. What I got from your draft is that sociology helps us understand our relationships with other people and lead better lives. But it wasn't until the end of the essay that I began to get that idea. I wonder if you weren't actually warmed up to your subject until near the end?

Part of your problem may be that your thesis is not specific enough. Half of it says that sociology is not only a class, but your essay doesn't develop that part of your thesis at all. So the part that refers to what you do say is only "it's a vital force of life." Can you make that more specific—to specify, maybe, what it is about sociology class that makes it so vital?

Once you clarify your thesis, you will probably be able to see your paragraphs in a fresh light. Your second paragraph, for example, seems not to contribute anything to your thesis as it's now stated; but maybe after rewriting your thesis you will see a way to revise the paragraph so it lays some groundwork for the rest of the essay. Your other paragraphs, too, do not clearly show how sociology class is important to our lives. The idea is there but not stated so a reader can relate it to your thesis.

Maybe what you need as you revise your paragraphs is some way of linking each one to your thesis—with key words in an opening sentence, perhaps (once you've established them in your new thesis).

I marked some of the errors in your essay, but since this is a first draft I didn't try to catch everything. You do have some comma splices, fragments, and spelling errors. Also, make sure your pronouns have clear reference.

Good luck revising this draft. If you expand on the ideas you expressed in your concluding paragraph, I'm sure you will end up with a very good essay.

Exercise 3-2, p. 47. Using the correction symbols

Sample revision (corrections are underlined).

Tough Trip

In the northern states, traveling in the winter can be hazardous and frustrating. The roads and weather conditions may be perfectly clear when the traveler leaves home, but after a few days of visiting relatives or taking care of business, the conditions may have changed drastically. My family and I have experienced such problems often. Possibly the worst occurrence was last year after Christmas when we were returning from visiting our grandparents in Chicago.

The trip was particularly bad for the last fifty miles or so between the Illinois border and Milwaukee. While the highway going around Chicago was wet and messy, the road as we entered Wisconsin became snow-covered and slick. And the farther we drove into our home state, the worse the roads became. From the 65-mile-per-hour speed that was common on I-294 and I-94 in Illinois, the traffic slowed to 60, then to 55, continuing to drop to about 30 and 35. Even at 30 miles per hour, stopping was impossible. We just drove along slowly, hoping that there would be no need to stop. All along the way the shoulders were punctuated by cars and trucks that had tried to do something different than to plod along at a regular though agonizingly slow rate of speed. The closer we got to Milwaukee, the worse the conditions became.

The absolute worst occurred after we entered the city. Choosing to drive through downtown, thinking that those streets would most likely be cleared (and going that way was the most direct route to our house), we drove into a huge traffic snarl made up of cars, trucks, and buses stuck in and grinding away at the entire eight inches of damp, slushy, slippery, no-longer- white stuff occupying Jackson Street and Wisconsin Avenue. The plowing crews were waiting for people to go home so they could clear the streets, but the only way people could go home was to push their cars around the stuck ones and out of the slush.

After we got home and turned on the radio, we heard what we already had discovered: the storm had dumped eight inches of snow on Milwaukee in just a few hours, whereas areas to the south had received a mere two or three inches of snow, and farther to the south there was rain. After shoveling out the driveway and putting away the car, we were glad to be home.

CHAPTER 4

Writing and Revising Paragraphs

Exercise 4-1, p. 67. Identifying irrelevant details

1. Sentences 3 and 6 are irrelevant.
2. Sentences 4 and 5 are irrelevant.

Exercise 4-2, p. 68. Identifying the topic sentence

1. Topic sentence: "Diamonds are the hardest naturally occurring substance known."
2. Topic sentence: "So, even though diamonds are the hardest natural substance known, there are ways of destroying them."
3. Topic sentence: "Because of these facts, diamonds are sparklingly brilliant."
4. Topic sentence: "There are only four major sources of diamonds: Africa, India, Siberia, and South America."

Exercise 4-3, p. 69. Organizing paragraphs: Spatial order

Order of sentences: 1, 3, 8, 5, 7, 2, 4, 9, 6

Sample answer:

From head to foot he was clearly dressed for a Minnesota winter. A fur-lined parka covered his head and enveloped his wind-burned face, seeming to put his eyes at the end of a dark tunnel. His chin was somewhere beneath a plaid scarf that encircled his neck and lower face. Under the scarf his bulky coat—quilted, down-filled, an indistinct grayish brown—attached to the base of the parka. The coat was of the type that has an industrial-strength zipper hidden beneath a fly that fastens down with toggles. One of the toggle buttons was missing, leaving a creased gap that revealed the heavy zipper underneath. His thick coat sleeves ended in sheepskin mittens, the soft leather exposed to the outside, the furry interior wrapping and warming his hands. His legs were protected from the elements too, encased in lined and quilted pants of a vague greenish color. Finally, on his feet were heavy leather boots, laced up above his ankles, topped with the red-striped cuffs of his wool socks.

Exercise 4-4, p. 70. Organizing paragraphs: Chronological order

Order of sentences: 1, 3, 12, 5, 8, 2, 9, 7, 4, 10, 6, 11

Sample answer:

This is how I make my high-caloric, high-cholesterol, irresistible caramels. First, I get out all the ingredients: a pint of cream, a stick of butter, two cups of sugar, one cup of white corn syrup, a bit of salt, and the bottle of vanilla. Into a heavy saucepan I put the sugar, the corn syrup, one cup of the cream, and a dash of salt. I set the saucepan on medium heat and stir the mixture while it comes to a boil. Once it has begun to boil, I attach a candy thermometer to the side of the pan, turn the heat down, and let the mixture cook to the soft-ball stage, about 235 degrees. Then I add the remaining cream, bringing the mixture to a boil again, and I cook it again to the soft-ball stage. At each soft-ball stage the mixture is a light brown color. When the soft- ball stage has been reached for the second time, I add the stick of butter and continue cooking until the mixture reaches almost 246 degrees. By now it has become a medium brown. I remove the saucepan from the heat, take out the thermometer, and stir in one teaspoon of vanilla. Quickly I pour the hot caramel mixture into a nine-by-nine-inch buttered pan and let it set to cool and become firm. Then I remove it from the pan and, with a large sharp knife, cut it into those melt-in-your-mouth, irresistible little cubes.

Exercise 4-5, p. 71. Organizing paragraphs: Specific to general

Order of sentences: 7, 2, 1, 5, 3, 4, 6

Sample answer:

The United States and its territories and possessions measure more than 3.6 million square miles. This entire area must be mapped in detail. In addition to maps covering different areas, maps are needed for many official purposes, both scientific and administrative. Furthermore, there is a great demand for maps for recreational purposes. Because of the large area to be covered and the various purposes people have for maps, the US Geological Survey issues about 65,000 different geological survey maps. Add to this number the multiple copies of the many kinds of the maps that are needed to meet public demand. The result is a warehouse stock in the US Department of the Interior of over 100 million maps.

Exercise 4-6, p. 72. Organizing paragraphs: Problem to solution

Order of sentences: 1, 10, 5, 4, 7, 3, 6, 8, 2, 9.

Sample answer:

Students often wonder how they can gain the experience necessary for a job when they haven't yet worked at that job. The fact is that the best-paying jobs do require experience. It's also a fact that students occupied with getting their education are not employed in their career field. Fortunately, there is some good news. One way that students can gain valuable experience is through internships offered through their colleges. Although internships may not pay much—and sometimes pay nothing at all—the experience and connections are like money in the bank. But what if you can't get an internship? Volunteer work is the answer. It pays nothing at all, but it's an opportunity for students to develop career-related skills. In addition to the skills gained, volunteers can develop a network of people who are familiar with the volunteers and who are acquainted with the employers looking for qualified applicants.

Exercise 4-7, p. 73. Organizing paragraphs: Climactic order

Order of sentences: 1, 6, 3, 8, 5, 4, 2, 7

Sample answer:

I could tell as I saw Dusty step onto the stack of papers that something terrible was about to happen. When she stepped up to the pile of books, leaving her back paws still on the paper, it began. First the papers started to slide, exposing beneath them the magazines and computer disks. The entire stack was immediately in motion, and Dusty began shifting her weight to the books. They too began to move. As the books quivered under her, the flowerpot with three little seedlings, sitting atop the books to catch the afternoon sun, lost its footing. Suddenly everything was in the air: papers, magazines, computer disks, books, flowerpot, and cat. When they crashed, it was in a pile of dirt—all except Dusty (she was nowhere to be found) and the seedlings (they were no more).

Exercise 4-8, p. 75. Being consistent

Sample revisions (changes are underlined):

1. According to the US Centers for Disease Control and Prevention, children can be exposed to the hazards of lead poisoning in many ways. In some cases, <u>the children could die</u>. <u>Their</u> exposure <u>can</u> come from nearby industrial sites, lead water pipes in older <u>houses</u>, lead-containing ceramics, some folk medicines, but most of all from lead-based paint in older houses. More than 890,000 American children have high <u>levels</u> of lead in their <u>blood streams</u>. In houses built before 1978, <u>children</u> can ingest lead by eating paint chips, breathing contaminated dust, or putting their hands in their <u>mouths</u> after touching contaminated dust. Remodeling projects often only exacerbate the problem.
2. There are three primary reasons for a person to need eyeglasses: myopia, hyperopia, and presbyopia. <u>A person</u> with myopia, known familiarly as nearsightedness, <u>sees</u> clearly up close but distant objects are blurred. This condition <u>appears</u> around puberty and <u>worsens</u> until the early 20s. You probably known somebody with this condition. Hyperopia is the opposite of myopia—in other words, farsightedness, in which distant objects are seen clearly but near objects <u>are</u> fuzzy. This condition usually doesn't appear until mid-life. It may not apply to you. And finally, in presbyopia <u>the eyes</u> gradually <u>lose</u> <u>their</u> ability to focus on near objects, creating the need for reading glasses, usually after age 45.

Exercise 4-9, p. 77. Arranging and linking sentences

Sample paragraph:

The greatest volcanic eruption of modern times occurred on August 27, 1883, when the island of Krakatoa, in what is now Indonesia, blew up. At first the island's mountains spewed rocks and ash into the air for a day, blackening the sky. The mountains exploded with a roar that could be heard three thousand miles away. The explosion also created winds that circled the earth several times. The island sank into the ocean, causing gigantic tidal waves that swallowed up coastal cities and inland towns. The tidal waves appeared finally as unusually large waves on the English coast, half a world away. When the earth calmed down again, almost nothing remained of the island. In the aftermath nearly forty thousand people were discovered to have died.

Exercise 4-10, p. 78. Using paragraph patterns of development

No sample answers.

Exercise 4-11, p. 79. Parallelism, repetition, pronouns, and transitional expressions: Identifying

1. a. in addition
   b. then
   c. further
   d. moreover
   e. but
2. a. sea creature, its, it, octopus, octopus's
   b. enemies, prey, it, anything, shells, prey, other creature, neighbors
3. a. tentacles
   b. home
   c. seabed
4. a. Noun: octopus — Pronoun: it, its
   b. Noun: prey — Pronoun: it
   c. Noun: brain — Pronouns: that
5. a. 2
   b. 3
   c. 8

Exercise 4-12, p. 81. Opening and closing an essay

Sample answers:

1. Introduction: statement of subject, background information.
   Conclusion: summary, restatement of thesis, question.
2. Introduction: historical fact, background information, statement of subject.
   Conclusion: summary, opinion.
3. Introduction: background information, statement of subject.
   Conclusion: opinion, quotation, suggestion of a course of action.

Exercise 4-13, p. 83. Analyzing an essay's coherence

Sample answer (repetitions are single underlined, parallels double underlined):

Sunny Days

1 There are many places in the world I would like to visit. Yet, if I could visit any place of my own choosing I would choose a place within the boundaries of the United States. It's a place everyone knows of, yet, no one quite knows how to get there. Still, through the power of imagination almost everyone has been there. This place is none other than *Sesame Street*.

2 *Sesame Street* is an amazing place that is full of wonder and magic. The heart of this wonder and magic is the street's innocence. It is not a place of perfection. The rules must be broken (but never on purpose) in order for a lesson to be learned. A toy might not be shared or feelings might be hurt, but everything always comes out all right in the end with a hug.

3 How I would love to walk the sidewalks of *Sesame Street*. I'd ride on the tire swing that hangs in the corner, right by the staircase. I'd visit Oscar in his trash can, and when he tells me to scram I would just smile. I'd say "Hi" to Big Bird and let him know that I always knew Mr. Snuffleupagus was true. I'd shake Bob's hand because he's Bob—one of the "People in My Neighborhood." Maybe I'd have a snack with Cookie Monster, or go counting with the Count. Before the end of the day, I might take my toaster over to the Fix-It Shop to be fixed. Then I'd "Dance Myself to Sleep" with Ernie.

4 *Sesame Street*'s appeal is unique. As a young child I first watched because it was something my parents put in front of me. It was a learning tool that gave me a jump start on all I would be exposed to once I was old enough for school. However, as the years went by it was I who would get up early in the morning on my own just to visit this street and my friends who lived there. But there comes a point when enough is enough. I eventually came to realize that I was too smart for *Sesame Street*. I refused to watch the show out of pride because I was sure I was so smart, even though I secretly still loved every minute of it. As time passed and I came to be in junior high, it once again became "OK" to like *Sesame Street*. I didn't watch it now, but there was no longer any reason to deny that Ernie was my favorite Muppet on the Street.

5 As an adult, not only do I continue to hold a special place in my heart for my *Sesame Street* friends, but I now realize how lucky I was to have them. Thanks to cable television I can watch and revisit the *Sesame Street* I saw as a kid; for the current Street is now home to many new monsters and other creatures whose names I don't even know. As I watch and experience what I laughed at as a small child, I now see that everything happened for a purpose. Each clever sketch had a lesson—about sharing or cooperation or whatever lesson a child may need to learn. I also see that *Sesame Street* has a certain appeal for adults. A young child sees just another person hanging out on the Street and singing; an adult sees Stevie Wonder singing a simple song he could sing only in the presence of Muppets. And all those conversations between Muppets and kids about color

of skin (or fur) meant much more than I was possibly able to comprehend. For this reason, I think the world could stand to revisit *Sesame Street* with me.

6 It's a place where everyone can feel at home, children and adults alike. Rubber Duckie is everyone's best friend, and there is the sudden urge to dance along with Bert anytime he's "Doin' the Pigeon." It's not always easy "Bein' Green," but you soon realize that what is most important is to be yourself and be proud of that person, no matter how hard it may be. Yes, this is where I'd like to visit. If even only for a day, that day would create an additional lifetime of memories to add to the ones I already have of *Sesame Street* and all who live there.

—Rosemary Reeve, student writer

II CRITICAL THINKING, READING, AND WRITING

CHAPTER 5

Taking a Critical Perspective

Exercise 5-1, p. 93. Reading for understanding

No sample answer.

Exercise 5-2, p. 97. Summarizing

1. a.
2. a.
3. No sample answer.

Exercise 5-3, p. 99. Reading critically—Analyzing, interpreting, synthesizing, evaluating

No sample answer.

Exercise 5-4, p. 101. Writing critically—Analyzing, interpreting, synthesizing, evaluating

No sample answer.

CHAPTER 6

Reading Arguments Critically

Exercise 6-1, p. 113. Testing claims

1.	2	6.	2	11.	2
2.	1	7.	3	12.	3
3.	2	8.	1	13.	2
4.	1	9.	3	14.	1
5.	1	10.	4	15.	1

Exercise 6-2, p. 114. Analyzing assumptions

Sample answers:

1. Killing a murderer somehow equalizes, or negates, the crime. Evidence needed.
2. Proponents of capital punishment favor killing. Evidence needed.
3. Murder is defined as any taking of human life. Evidence needed.
4. Parents must discipline their children. Evidence perhaps not needed.
5. Spanking is the same as hitting. Evidence needed.
6. Children must be disciplined. Evidence perhaps not needed.
7. There are hungry and homeless people in the locality. Evidence probably needed.
8. There are hungry and homeless people. Evidence probably needed.
9. Dolphins are being slaughtered. Evidence needed.
10. Dolphins have been killed. Evidence needed.

Exercise 6-3, p. 115. Examining evidence

Sample answers:

Facts: "Whatever one thinks of investment banking or corporate law, the perks and the pay are way ahead of those for waitressing and data entry."
Statistics: "In medicine, law and management, they [women] have increased their participation by 300% to 400% since the early '70s."
Examples: Paragraph 4 sentences beginning "Women...."
Expert opinions: "Women don't want to exchange places with men."
Appeals to readers' beliefs or needs: "The hand that rocks the cradle—and cradles the phone, and sweeps the floor, and writes the memo and meets the deadline—doesn't have time to reach out and save the world."

Exercise 6-4, p. 119. Identifying logical fallacies

Sample answers:

1. Question begging
2. Reductive fallacy
3. Hasty generalization, stereotype
4. Argument *ad populum*
5. Flattery
6. *Post hoc* fallacy
7. Hasty generalization, stereotype
8. Reductive fallacy
9. Hasty generalization
10. Either/or fallacy
11. Hasty generalization, stereotype, *non sequitur*
12. Either/or fallacy, question begging
13. Argument *ad hominem*
14. Bandwagon, flattery
15. Hasty generalization
16. False analogy, reductive fallacy
17. False analogy
18. *Non sequitur*
19. Either/or fallacy
20. Question begging, *non sequitur*

CHAPTER 7

Writing an Argument

Exercise 7-1, p. 129. Analyzing an argument

No sample answers.

III USING COMPUTERS CRITICALLY

CHAPTER 8

Becoming Computer Literate

Exercise 8-1, p. 137. Using your word processor

No sample answers.

Exercise 8-2, p. 138 Using electronic mail

No sample answer.

CHAPTER 9

Designing Documents

Exercise 9-1, p. 143. Designing documents

No sample answers.

CHAPTER 10

Composing for the Web

No exercise.

CHAPTER 11

Collaborating Online

Exercise 11-1, p. 149. Using online collaboration

No sample answers.

IV GRAMMATICAL SENTENCES

CHAPTER 12

Understanding Sentence Grammar

Exercise 12-1, p. 175. Subjects and predicates: Identifying and comparing

1. The most common cow in the United States | is the Holstein.
2. About 70 percent of the dairy cattle in this country | are Holsteins.
3. You | have probably seen these large black and white cows grazing beside the highway.
4. The origin of this breed of cattle | is Northern Europe, specifically Friesland.
5. They | were later raised also in Holstein, an area of Germany.
6. Dutch settlers | probably brought the first Holstein cattle to the United States in the early 1600s.
7. Somewhat smaller than Holsteins, Guernseys | are a light brown, almost golden, with white markings.
8. These dairy cattle | were developed on the Isle of Guernsey in the English Channel and did not arrive in the United States until the early 1800s.
9. Jersey, another island in the English Channel, | is the namesake of the Jersey cow.
10. The Jerseys | probably migrated to that island across a land bridge from Europe.
11. Jersey cows | are fawn-colored and have an interesting muzzle: black encircled by a light ring.
12. These three breeds—Holsteins, Guernseys, and Jerseys— | make up most of the milk-producing cattle in the United States.
13. Their ability to produce large quantities of milk | makes them popular with dairy producers.

Exercise 12-2, p. 177. Nouns, verbs, and pronouns: Identifying functions

```
            N              N             V         N
1.  Most people in the United States remember carnivals from
               N                     N                       N
    their* childhood and youthful years.  These traveling shows
        V       N       N            N       P    V
    included rides, sideshows, and games.  They were sometimes
     V                 N        N                          N
    set up in parking lots at malls as ways to attract customers
                          N           N
    and sometimes in fairgrounds as part of county or state
      N        N      V     V     P          N
    fairs.  People would attend them for amusement and
```

```
    N                              N               N
diversion, occasionally winning prizes for their games of
  N
skill.

                      N      V     N          N       P     V
2.  Historically, carnivals are periods of feasting that precede
            N          N     P               V
    the beginning of Lent.  They sometimes begin early in the
          N          V                     N         N
    new year and continue until Shrove Tuesday, the day before
           N                                N      V   V
    Ash Wednesday.  These celebratory carnivals may have
         V                 N           P     V
    originated in ancient Egypt, and they were common in ancient
     N                    N     P     V      V
    Rome.  In the Middle Ages they were assimilated by the Roman
                N          V                  N             N
    Catholic Church and took on religious overtones.  Carnivals
     V                     N         N                    N
    are still common in parts of Europe, and in this country
      P    V                  N            N
    they exist at the Mardi Gras in New Orleans.

                            N       V    N
3.  Common to amusement carnivals are rides, those mechanical
       N     P     V      N              N       N
    devices that give pleasure through speed, height, or
                    N                  N     V  N
    unaccustomed motion.  The Ferris wheel is one of these
      N     P  V                   N     P      V
    rides.  It is a large upright wheel that rotates and
        V        N                N             N
    transports people from the ground to an elevation high above
            N                                           N     V
    the carnival and then down again.  Occasionally riders are
         V              N          N                      N
    suspended at the top or in midair on the downward slope
             N         V        V                    N
    while passengers exit and enter at the ground level.  This
               N     V    P    N                N
    popular wheel takes its name from G. W. Ferris, its
        N      P     V             N                         N
    inventor, who built the first one for the 1893 World's Fair
          N       P  V              N            N
    in Chicago.  It was a double wheel with a capacity of 2000
       N
    riders.
```

*Words like their, your, and man's function as adjectives, modifying the nouns that follow them.

Exercise 12-3, p. 179. Nouns and verbs: Writing sentences

No sample answers.

Exercise 12-4, p. 181. Parts of the sentence: Identifying

S V
1. Bats live a long time.
S V
2. Bamboo plants grow for many years without flowering.
S V V V
3. Some varieties of fish cluck, croak, or grunt.
S V V
4. Sound waves must travel through a medium.
S
5. Some unanswered questions about quark matter still
V
remain.
S V V DO
6. Some foods may increase chances of getting cancer.
S V V DO
7. However, other foods may provide an effective means of preventing the disease.
S V DO
8. Pandas eat almost nothing except bamboo.
S V DO
9. Computer camps offer computer training in a camplike setting.
S V DO
10. Scientists group butterflies into families according to their physical features.
S V SC
11. Freon is a common cooling agent.
S V SC
12. Bats are intriguing creatures because of their unusual characteristics.
S V SC
13. The Doppler effect is an apparent change in pitch.
S V SC
14. Infrasound means sound with frequencies below the range of human hearing.
S V SC
15. The sun's rays are strongest between 10:00 AM and 2:00 PM.
S V IO DO
16. A male frog sends a female frog a hoarse mating call.
S V V IO DO
17. Zoo officials sometimes must feed baby animals milk from a bottle.
S V IO DO
18. Medical technologists very seldom give people high doses of ionizing radiation.
S V V IO DO
19. Trilobites have given paleontologists evidence of continent formation.
S V

20. According to some botanists, trees sometimes send other
IO DO
trees chemical messages when under attack by insects.

S V DO DO OC
21. Scientists call butterflies and moths Lepidoptera.

S V DO OC
22. They sometimes call computers "artificial intelligence."

S V DO OC
23. Some botanists consider the Cretaceous period the time of
the first flowers.

S V V DO
24. Environmentalists have declared the spread of airborne
OC
pollutants a major environmental concern.

S V V DO
25. Physicians have named some birth defects "fetal alcohol
OC
syndrome."

Exercise 12-5, p. 183. Sentence patterns: Combining sentences

Sample answers:

1. The enormous Mayan pyramids still stand today.
2. Mayan and other Indian tribes settled El Salvador as early as 3000 BC.
3. El Salvador's climate is agreeable, the average year-round temperature ranging from 73 to 80 degrees Fahrenheit.
4. The climate gives El Salvadorans an opportunity to play soccer on soccer fields throughout the country.
5. Spain made El Salvador a Spanish colony in 1524.

Exercise 12-6, p. 185. Adjectives and adverbs: Identifying function

1. Water conservation is becoming an urgent issue.
2. Some areas of the United States have severe water shortages, while others have abundant sources of drinkable water.
3. California, Arizona, and other parts of the Southwest are particularly affected by severe shortages.
4. As people continually move to areas where there is less water, the situation becomes increasingly dire.
5. There are numerous reasons for population growth in areas where water is scarce.

6. People want to live in a warm, sunny climate where they don't have to be inconvenienced occasionally by rain and snow.

7. The Sunbelt is attractive to industry too.

8. But the Southwest commonly has low precipitation and, because of the heat, high evaporation.

9. To make matters worse, the lengthy growing seasons encourage farmers to plant more crops and irrigate them copiously.

10. Scientists estimate that the average person uses approximately 140 gallons of water every day.

11. They further estimate that, for each person in the country, an additional 740 gallons are used every day for agriculture and another 700 gallons for industry.

12. One solution is to use snow melt from nearby mountains to irrigate fields.

13. Another solution is removal of saline from ocean water.

14. Still another answer has been to dam rivers and divert the flow to needy areas.

15. Unfortunately, there is only so much water, and even mighty rivers like the Colorado cannot meet the demand of the Southwest.

16. Even aquifers, those underground rock formations that yield fresh, clean water to deep wells, are fast being depleted by overuse.

17. Some parts of the country have abundant sources of water such as the Great Lakes, the Mississippi, and other rivers.

18. But getting potable water from places where it is plentiful to areas where it is scarce is a problem that has not been satisfactorily solved.

19. Neither have we discovered a practical and inexpensive way of desalinating sea water in amounts adequate to serve the need.

Exercise 12-7, p. 187. Prepositions: Writing sentences

Original sentences will vary.

1. In a book by Mary Karr called *The Liars' Club*, the life in an East Texas refinery town in the 1960s looks distinctly unattractive.
2. The future for space stations is uncertain, especially in today's economic climate.
3. People should view solar eclipses only with proper eye protection.
4. In one school of thought, life on earth began somewhere else in the universe.
5. Contrary to other liquids, water freezes from the top.
6. At the surface of the hottest star, the temperature might be 200,000 degrees Fahrenheit.
7. Passover is a Jewish holiday celebrated from the fourteenth to the twenty-second of Nisan in the Jewish calendar, or sometime in March or April.
8. Quartz clocks use the vibrations of quartz crystals driving a motor at a precise rate.
9. With the increase of pollution after World War II, unrestrained waste and use of chemicals were seen by many people as a threat to the planet.
10. The Centers for Disease Control and Prevention based in Atlanta, Georgia, provides consultation on an international basis for the control of preventable diseases.

Exercise 12-8, p. 189. Prepositional phrases: Identifying function

As you drive (along the highway) (in the country), you often see beef cattle grazing (in pastures). (In contrast) (to dairy cows), which are raised (for milk production), beef cattle are raised (for their meat) and are much larger. Three major breeds (of beef cattle) (in the United States) are Black Angus, Charolais, and Hereford. The Black Angus, or Aberdeen Angus, originated (in eastern Scotland) (in the county) (of Angus). The Black Angus is readily identifiable (by its smooth, black coat). It was first imported (to the United States) (in the late 1800s). The Charolais is a fairly recent import, having come (to this country) (by way) (of Mexico) (in 1936). The breed originated (in France). Charolais cattle are white, and they grow quite large, an adult bull being almost twice the size (of a Jersey milk cow), (for example). Herefords were developed (in Herefordshire, England,) and were brought (to the United States) (in the early 1800s). These beef cattle have white faces, reddish coats, and white markings. (In addition) (to these major breeds) (of beef cattle), two other types are common: the Redpoll and the Shorthorn. These two are used (for both dairy and beef production).

Exercise 12-9, p. 190. Participles: Using *-ing* and *-ed*

1.	interesting	5.	guiding	9.	dedicated
2.	supposed	6.	deteriorating	10.	declining
3.	surprising	7.	burning	11.	intriguing
4.	unknown	8.	distinguishing	12.	acquired

Exercise 12-10, p. 191. Verbal phrases: Identifying function

1. i, DO (of asked)
2. i, DO (of have)
3. g, S
4. g, OP (of besides)
5. g, OP (of When)
6. g, S
7. i, OP (of for)
8. i, adj. (modifying the angle)
9. g, OP (of What)
10. i, adv. (modifying the verb make)
11. g, OP (of of)
12. i, adv. (modifying the verb make)
13. i, DO (of find; exciting is an object complement)
14. g, OP (of by)
15. g, S (of the verb lets), i, DO (of the verb lets)
16. p, adj. (modifying They)
17. p, adj. (modifying they)
18. i, SC (renaming errors)
19. p, adj. (modifying others [the entire phrase is an absolute])
20. g, OP (of for)

Exercise 12-11, p. 193. Verbal phrases: Revising sentences

Sample answers:

1. Oceans are the home of many of earth's creatures, *covering 70 percent of the earth's surface.*
2. The oceans, *all interconnected*, are named Pacific, Indian, Atlantic, and Arctic.
3. The continental shelves are the parts of the oceans *best known.*
4. Most commercial fishing is done here, *the waters being relatively shallow.*
5. Although *making up a major part of the earth*, the ocean is still largely unknown.
6. For most people, the very edge of the ocean is the part *known best.*
7. They like going to the beach *to absorb the sights and sounds of the ocean.*
8. Oceanographers spend their lives studying the oceans *to know its riches and its perils.*
9. *To get a comprehensive view of the ocean environment*, they study geography, ecology, physics, chemistry, marine biology, and meteorology.
10. *When going to the beach next time*, think of the ocean as the habitat for creatures *sharing the planet with you.*

Exercise 12-12, p. 195. Subordinate clauses: Identifying function

1. n, OP
2. adv, modifies occurs
3. n, DO
4. adj, modifies rates
5. adj, modifies women
6. n, SC
7. adj, modifies campaigns
8. adj, modifies administrators
9. adj, modifies ones
10. adj, modifies means
11. adj, modifies brochures
12. adv, modifies change
13. adv, modifies made
14. adj, modifies force
15. n, SC

Exercise 12-13, p. 197. Subordinate clauses: Combining sentences

Sample answers:

1. When it first came out in 1888, the *National Geographic* had no pictures.
2. Though it was rather plain in its beginnings, it is now one of the most colorful of magazines.
3. Gilbert H. Grosvenor, who founded the National Geographic Society, was its president for fifty-five years.
4. Subscribers, who are called "members," number 10.5 million.
5. The *National Geographic* has published reports from adventurers who have traveled all over the world.
6. Although the written reports are often interesting and exciting, it is the pictures that attract many readers.
7. Because the *Geographic* has published colorful pictures from distant lands, its readers know a little about the culture of many peoples.
8. Its readers have firsthand accounts from explorers who have traveled to exotic places.
9. A familiar explorer who recorded his underwater travels was Jacques Cousteau.
10. Reinhold Messner was another *National Geographic* explorer who made history when he climbed to the top of Mt. Everest.
11. Many explorers have received research support from the Society, which has an annual budget of more than $5 million.

Exercise 12-14, p. 199. Subordinate clauses: Writing sentences

Original sentences will vary.

1. Some people wonder whether vitamin supplements are good for their health.
2. In fact, vitamins might be more important than people once thought.
3. It has been surmised that some vitamins might ward off cancer and heart disease.
4. Vitamin C, which was once suggested for fighting colds, may instead reduce risk of cancer and heart disease.

5. Vitamin A, or beta carotene, may reduce the risk of many kinds of cancer that are common to either men or women.
6. Because all vitamins are found in foods, the best source of these nutrients is naturally in our food.
7. Vitamin C is best found in citrus fruits; beta carotene, which converts to Vitamin A in the body, is available in dark green leafy vegetables.
8. People who do not regularly eat a balanced diet might be better off taking a comprehensive vitamin supplement.
9. At the same time, they should be aware that vitamin pills do not provide all the nutrients of food.
10. Proteins, carbohydrates, and fiber are three examples of essential nutrients that are not available in vitamin pills.
11. Even though scientists do not fully understand the additional, lesser known nutrients, they recognize their value.
12. The answer seems to be that vitamin pills have value mainly as supplements to a regular balanced diet.

Exercise 12-15, p. 201. Compound constructions: Revising clauses

Sample answers:

1. Madison is the capital of Wisconsin, but Milwaukee is the largest city.
   Madison is the capital of Wisconsin; however, Milwaukee is the largest city.
2. In summer Wisconsin's lakes attract swimmers and boaters, and in winter they attract iceboaters and snowmobilers.
   In summer Wisconsin's lakes attract swimmers and boaters; then in winter they attract iceboaters and snowmobilers.
3. Wisconsin is the nation's leading milk producer, so it is called "America's dairyland."
   Wisconsin is the nation's leading milk producer; consequently, it is called "America's dairyland."
4. Wisconsin's cities are mainly Democratic, but its rural areas are largely Republican.
   Wisconsin's cities are mainly Democratic; however, its rural areas are largely Republican.
5. Milwaukee was once a fur-trading center, but now it is known for its manufacturing.
   Milwaukee was once a fur-trading center; in contrast, now it is known for its manufacturing.
6. Milwaukee is known also for its variety of ethnic cultures, yet most of its residents were born in the United States.
   Milwaukee is known also for its variety of ethnic cultures; nevertheless, most of its residents were born in the United States.
7. The Wisconsin climate is characterized by warm summers and severely cold winters, but along the lake shorelines the temperatures are somewhat modified.
   The Wisconsin climate is characterized by warm summers and severely cold winters; however, along the lake shorelines the temperatures are somewhat modified.
8. The Lake Michigan shoreline is a fly path for migrating birds, so bird watchers flock to eastern Wisconsin every spring and fall.
   The Lake Michigan shoreline is a fly path for migrating birds; therefore, bird watchers flock to eastern Wisconsin every spring and fall.
9. Jean Nicolet, a French explorer, landed on the shore of Green Bay in 1634, so he is said to be the first European to set foot in Wisconsin.
   Jean Nicolet, a French explorer, landed on the shore of Green Bay in 1634; consequently, he is said to be the first white person to set foot in Wisconsin.

10. The Ringling Brothers started their first circus in Baraboo, Wisconsin, in 1884, and the Circus World Museum there commemorates this event with circus memorabilia.
The Ringling Brothers started their first circus in Baraboo, Wisconsin, in 1884; accordingly, the Circus World Museum there commemorates this event with circus memorabilia.

Exercise 12-16, p. 203. Compound constructions: Combining words and phrases

Sample answers:

1. The sun's rays strike the earth at a 90-degree angle at the equator and at acute angles at the poles.
2. Hurricane Andrew uprooted trees and destroyed homes.
3. Forecasters analyze reports from hurricane hunters and learn where the hurricane's center is located.
4. Hurricane hunters are US Air Force and Navy pilots.
5. Methods of weather forecasting differ in the kinds of maps used and in the details given.
6. To forecast weather, meteorologists must know present and past conditions.
7. High-pressure winds blow clockwise in the Northern Hemisphere and counterclockwise in the Southern Hemisphere.
8. Precipitation is water droplets and ice crystals that fall to earth.
9. Clouds and steady rain or snow precede the arrival of a warm front.
10. Much of the sun's energy is absorbed by the earth and changed into heat.

Exercise 12-17, p. 205. Order of sentences: Rewriting sentences

Sample answers:

1. Almost everyone has accepted computers as part of everyday life.
2. Decision makers call on computer specialists for assistance.
3. Most people have come to expect the speed of computer transactions.
4. Computers complete long-distance telephone calls in a matter of seconds.
5. Computers make airline and other reservations almost immediately.
6. To forget what life was like before computers is easy.
7. Inexpensive computer programs are being marketed.
8. Some programs are still costly.
9. The newer and more specialized programs are costly.
10. Many people depend on computers for survival on the job.

Exercise 12-18, p. 207. Compound, complex, and compound-complex sentences: Writing

No sample answers.

CHAPTER 13

Case of Nouns and Pronouns

Exercise 13-1, p. 217. Pronoun case: Compound subjects and objects

1.	her	5.	him	9.	he
2.	he	6.	She	10.	he
3.	She	7.	She	11.	he
4.	they	8.	him	12.	him

Exercise 13-2, p. 219. Pronoun case: *Who* and *Whom*

Sample answers:

1. Who will be the new dean?
2. Whom does this car belong to? *or* To whom does this car belong?
3. Whom can we count on to work at the hospital?
4. Whom can I ask about organic gardening?
5. Who was the last person to leave the room?
6. Whom should I call if I'm delayed?
7. To whom should applicants send their checks? *or* Whom should applicants send their checks to?
8. Whom can we ask to make the sign?

Exercise 13-3, p. 221. Pronoun case: Review

1.	your	7.	I	13.	Whom
2.	us	8.	We	14.	his
3.	whoever	9.	me	15.	whom
4.	We	10.	Whom	16.	Who
5.	I	11.	who	17.	whom
6.	whoever	12.	who	18.	whom, who

Exercise 13-4, p. 223. Pronoun case: Rewriting a text

Sample answers (changes are underlined):

Sherlynn decided to drive out to Laramie, Wyoming, by herself last June to visit her sister Laura and her family. No one could have been more surprised at the turn of events than she! From her departure in Minnesota to her arrival in Wyoming, there was one incident after another.

Like any careful car owner, she had her car serviced before she left—oil changed and the whole deal. She even had it washed—the super duper deluxe treatment. Then, because there was a good chance of rain over the next couple of days, she and her nextdoor neighbor applied Rain-X to her windshield so she'd have less trouble seeing the road during downpours.

As they anticipated, there was rain. In fact, it rained the entire first day. But at least the Rain-X worked: the raindrops beaded off her windshield with little help from the wipers. And at least it wasn't hot. She was comfortable in a tee shirt and lightweight jeans. She stopped overnight at a small town in South Dakota, where she found a little restaurant that served locally grown beef—plus something that kept her and her stomach awake all night. Before turning in, she spent some time walking along the dusty streets to remind her legs that they still had a function other than taking over from the cruise control whenever called upon.

The next day she drove through the Badlands—VERY impressive as dirt piles go! Then of course it was important for her to see the Black Hills. The landscape there is lovely, but she skipped a close-up of Mount Rushmore because the parking lot was too full. Driving away from the area, she was sorry to leave the dark green hills behind but had no regrets about getting away from all the people.

Did I tell you that the air-conditioning in the car had quit working the day she left? Now the weather was turning hot as she struck out into western South Dakota, and she was getting quite uncomfortable, even in shorts and tee shirt. So her attitude was not good when she entered a construction zone and freshly applied blacktop. Her attitude did not improve when a passing truck kicked up a rock onto her windshield and cracked it—a jagged, six-inch gash near the wipers. Her mental totaling of the repair bill—air conditioner and now windshield—was damaging her confidence in herself as an intrepid traveler.

Well, she made it to Laramie, and she did enjoy herself. One day, she and Laura drove up into the mountains, and the air was cold. In fact, they noticed that most of the hiking trails were still snow-covered. Was the trip worth the trouble? It was, but the car seemed a little unhappy about the trip to the repair shop.

CHAPTER 14

Verbs

Exercise 14-1, p. 247. Principal parts of irregular verbs: Comparing forms

1.	swum	11.	worn	21.	laid
2.	come	12.	gone	22.	cut
3.	written	13.	threw	23.	torn
4.	drunk	14.	sat	24.	taken
5.	saw	15.	eaten	25.	given
6.	run	16.	seen	26.	frozen
7.	lain	17.	ridden	27.	rang
8.	begun	18.	fallen	28.	done
9.	chosen	19.	known	29.	broken
10.	driven	20.	grew	30.	sung

Exercise 14-2, p. 249. The *-s* forms of verbs: Rewriting a text

It is still thought necessary for people to drink eight glasses of water a day. Water, it is said, keeps the body functioning, nourished, and cool. Water makes up about 60 percent of the human body, and that level has to be maintained for good health. The water that leaves the body through the normal processes of perspiration and urination needs to be replenished.

About 7 percent of the body's water content circulates in the bloodstream. If the volume of water in the body drops, so does the volume of blood that circulates throughout the body. This decrease is accompanied by a corresponding increase in the chemical substances in the blood. The brain begins to get the message that water is necessary and sends a message of thirstiness to the mouth. By this time the body has already begun dehydrating.

What does dehydration mean? If the person ignores the call for water, it possibly means headaches, fatigue, muscle cramps, and mental dullness. In hot weather, the body temperature rises, because the natural cooling process of perspiration is stymied. In the long term, the person risks kidney damage.

These problems can be avoided if people drink lots of water. Because alcohol and caffeinated cola, tea, and coffee flush water out of the body, they counteract the benefits of the liquid they introduce. But water excels. It is almost free and has no calories.

Exercise 14-3, p. 251. The *-ed* forms of verbs: Rewriting a text

Sample answers:

When I was learning to write, my dictionary was always a close companion. I referred to it throughout the writing process for several purposes. Before I started writing, I often looked up the meaning of a key word so that I clearly understood my subject. At that time I also located related words and checked their meanings.

I probably referred to the dictionary least while I carried out the actual writing. At that time my writing so absorbed my thoughts that I overlooked spelling and, when I couldn't think of the right word, I used any word that came close in meaning. I placed a mark in the margin as a reminder to myself that I needed to find a different word later.

After I affixed my last period, I prepared to dig into my dictionary. Then I asked myself if each word I used was appropriate for my meaning. If I had any doubt, I looked up the word and checked its meaning. At that point, I also investigated other words given as synonyms; if they seemed better than the ones I had, I used them instead. As I revised, I also checked the spellings of words I was not sure about.

My final use for the dictionary occurred when I was writing the final draft. I needed to know how to divide words at the ends of lines. My dictionary had little dots between syllables to tell me where the syllables divided.

Because my dictionary was so useful to me while I wrote, I kept it handy all the time.

Exercise 14-4, p. 253. Helping verbs and main verbs: Comparing forms

1. considered
2. painted
3. entertain
4. work
5. start
6. have covered
7. apply
8. use
9. color, make
10. scared
11. have been
12. recommend
13. are made
14. exaggerates
15. painted

Exercise 14-5, p. 255. Sequence of tenses: Rewriting a text

Sample answers:

English was the dominant language for doing business in the world. It had become the second language of choice in regions that varied as widely as Southeast Asia and continental Europe. But even though there had been agreement on the language, there were still differences of opinion on which English to learn.

The two dominant forms of English were British and American. British was taught in most of Europe, Africa, and Russia, but American had grown more common in Latin America and Japan. In Canada and Southeast Asia you were likely to find both in somewhat equal mixtures.

Both forms of English had their roots in early Anglo-Saxon, and both essentially maintained the same syntax, or grammar. But in vocabulary, pronunciation, and spelling you could find variations. If you wanted to describe a particular kind of vehicle in England, you called it a *lorry*, but in America you called it a *truck*. As for pronunciation, England had various dialects just as the United States did. We had all heard of *Cockney* in British English and *Southern* in American. Spelling might have presented the greatest complications in international business for people who were troubled by inconsistencies such as *centre* (British) and *center* (American) or *colour* (British) and *color* (American).

If you were new to the United States and had learned English under the British system, American English might have presented some complications. To have become familiar with one dialect could have made another one sound strange. You might have needed to listen a little more closely to the accent and vocabulary of the Americans.

Exercise 14-6, p. 257. Gerunds and infinitives: Using as appropriate

1.	attending	8.	to eat
2.	to go	9.	to go
3.	to wait	10.	having
4.	failing	11.	to buy
5.	to wait	12.	to use
6.	to leave	13.	to practice
7.	eating	14.	to get
15	to help	17.	knowing
16.	going	18.	making

Exercise 14-7, p. 259. Two-word verbs: Understanding meaning

Sample answers:

1.	encountered	8.	consider
2.	reading	9.	rewrite
3.	submitting	10.	omitted
4.	correct	11.	discard
5.	discovered	12.	add
6.	presented	13.	submit
7.	introduced	14.	retrieved

Exercise 14-8, p. 261. Verb tenses: Writing sentences

1. has led
   Past: Scientific truth about the human brain led to untrue assumptions.
   Present: Scientific truth about the human brain leads to untrue assumptions.
2. is, exists
   Past, past: One misinterpretation was that artistic, or visual, ability existed only in the right half of the brain.
   Present perfect, present: One misinterpretation has been that artistic, or visual, ability exists only in the right half of the brain.

3. assumed, took
Present, present: People assume, falsely, that only the left half of the brain takes on analytical, logical tasks and only the right half creative and visual work.
Past perfect, past: People had assumed, falsely, that only the left half of the brain took on analytical, logical tasks and only the right half creative and visual work.

4. has shown
Present: But further research shows the left brain to be just as perceptive visually as the right brain.
Past: But further research showed the left brain to be just as perceptive visually as the right brain.

5. is, controls
Present perfect, present: The primary distinction between the two halves of the brain has been that the left brain controls language.
Past, past: The primary distinction between the two halves of the brain was that the left brain controlled language.

6. has
Past: In most people, only the left brain had the ability to name objects.
Past perfect: In most people, only the left brain had had the ability to name objects.

7. recognizes, does(n't) have
Present perfect, present: The right brain has recognized those objects but doesn't have a name for them.
Past perfect, past: The right brain had recognized those objects but didn't have a name for them.

8. are connected
Future: The left brain and right brain will be connected to one another by the corpus collosum, a thick band of nerve fibers.
Future perfect: The left brain and right brain will have been connected to one another by the corpus collosum, a thick band of nerve fibers.

9. send
Future: Through this bundle of nerves the two halves of the brain will send information to one another.
Present perfect: Through this bundle of nerves the two halves of the brain have sent information to one another.

10. is
Present perfect: Because of this connection, it has been a misinterpretation of scientific evidence to call a person "left-brained" or "right-brained."
Future: Because of this connection, it will be a misinterpretation of scientific evidence to call a person "left-brained" or "right-brained."

Exercise 14-9, p. 263. Subjunctive verb forms: Rewriting sentences

1.	write	5.	were
2.	were	6.	were
3.	were	7.	were
4.	pay	8.	were

Exercise 14-10, p. 265. Verb forms, tense, and mood: Editing a text

Don't get me wrong. I'm all for a clean environment—recycling, reducing pollution, and all that. But my sister ~~do~~ **does** go overboard—just a bit. My biggest problem is that she's a birdwatcher. Have you ever ~~rode~~ **ridden** in a car ~~drove~~ **driven** by a birdwatcher? It's not something you'd get ~~use~~ **used** to.

First, her car is full of what she ~~call~~ **calls** birding gear. She ~~gots~~ **has** binoculars, a book full of bird pictures that she ~~call~~ **calls** a field guide, a notebook that she ~~say~~ **says** is her birding journal, and, believe it or not, a vest kind of like those fishing vests with about a million pockets. I ~~look~~ **looked** at that vest once. What I ~~see~~ **saw** ~~is~~ **was** a pen in a little pocket just the shape of a pen, a tablet in another pocket, a big white handkerchief in another one, and I don't know what else.

The really scary part of riding in the car with my sister ~~happen~~ **happens** when we ~~going~~ **are going** down the road. Wherever we are, whatever the traffic, if she ~~see~~ **sees** a bird she stops. She just ~~slammed~~ **slams** on the brakes and stops—right in the middle of the road. Yesterday we ~~driving~~ **were driving** in to school and she ~~see~~ **saw** a big bird flying overhead. A HERON!" she ~~yells,~~ **yelled** and there we ~~are,~~ **were** stopped in the middle of the street. Cars ~~are~~ **were** honking their horns behind us, and she just calmly ~~pulls~~ **pulled** out her binoculars to take a close look at that bird. I should ~~of~~ **have** taken over the wheel.

Well, you see what I mean. Anyone that devoted to birdwatching is a menace. I'll keep recycling cans, but caring for every bird in the sky is not my business.

Exercise 14-11, p. 267. Active and passive voices: Revising text

Sample answers (new sentences are underlined):

Bulimia is an eating disorder common to an estimated 18 percent of the female population in high school and college. People with this binge-and-purge disorder consume large amounts of junk food and then force themselves to vomit it up. Sometimes they take laxatives or diuretics as a means of purging the body. Usually they do the bingeing in secret because the bulimics are ashamed of their habit. Yet the young woman, as a result of her conviction that she is fat, usually repeats the bingeing and purging.

Only in recent years have medical journals described bulimia separately from another eating disorder, anorexia nervosa. Since 1980, doctors have considered bulimia a psychiatric illness. However, even though the causes of the bingeing and then purging are psychiatric, the effects of the purging are largely physical.

Frequent purging of the body with vomiting, laxatives, or diuretics reduces the amount of an essential chemical in the body—potassium. Insufficient potassium may cause muscle weakness, even paralysis and kidney disease. The frequent purging might even affect the teeth because of the acidity of the stomach fluids.

Treatment of bulimia usually involves both medical doctors and psychiatrists. They sometimes recommend hospitalization, and treatment often lasts for months and years. Early medical consultation can often prevent the disorder.

CHAPTER 15

Agreement

Exercise 15-1, p. 279. Subjects and verbs: Editing sentences

1.	is	11.	is	21.	get
2.	were	12.	were spread	22.	eats
3.	requires	13.	are	23.	need
4.	enjoys	14.	C	24.	C, C
5.	are	15.	was		
6.	C	16.	ride, C		
7.	is	17.	is		
8.	are	18.	show, C		
9.	were	19.	C, play		
10.	was	20.	C, is		

Exercise 15-2, p. 283. Subjects and verbs: Rewriting sentences

1. Stars are giant balls of glowing gas.
2. Stars shine both day and night, even though they are visible only at night.
3. Meteors look like falling stars but are really pieces of rock or metal.
4. Double stars consist of pairs of stars.
5. Quasars send out strong radio waves.
6. The lives of stars are billions of years.
7. Astronomers get information about the lives of stars by studying star clusters.
8. After stars begin to shine, they start to change slowly.
9. The speeds of this process depend on the masses of the stars.
10. Photometers measure the brightness of stars.
11. A sound is caused by vibrations traveling through the air.
12. A sound vibration travels in waves.
13. An animal hears sounds that a human does not hear.
14. Pitch affects the loudness of a sound.
15. An echo is produced by sound waves striking a reflecting surface.
16. A bat makes a high-pitched sound as it flies in the dark.
17. A microphone changes sound waves into an electric current.
18. The human ear hears sounds with frequencies ranging from 20 to 20,000 vibrations a second.
19. The highest tone on a piano has a frequency of about 4000 vibrations a second.
20. Sound travels faster through a dense substance than through a less dense one.

Exercise 15-3, p. 285. Subject-verb agreement: Review

One of the symbols of our nation ~~consist~~ **consists** of sticks tied in a bundle. These sticks represent the individual states, and the bundle ~~represent~~ **represents** the United States. The symbol, like our flag, makes a statement. The symbol means "United we stand; divided we fall." The symbol and the statement ~~comes~~ **come** from an old story, one of the fables told by an ancient Greek storyteller named Aesop. In this story, a man ~~have~~ **has** several sons who are always quarreling with one another. The father, with frequent admonitions, ~~try~~ **tries** to get the sons to stop their arguing and fighting. But nothing works. Finally, the father ~~decide~~ **decides** to give his sons a practical lesson in the effects of disunity. He ~~ask~~ **asks** them to bring him a bundle of sticks. Handing the bundle to each of his sons, he tells them to break it in two shorter pieces. Each of the sons ~~try~~ **tries** to break the bundle, but none of them ~~are~~ **is** able to do so. There is too much strength when the sticks ~~has~~ **have** been tied together. Next the father unties the bundle and ~~hand~~ **hands** a single stick to each of his sons and ~~ask~~ **asks** each son to break his stick. Of course, all of the sons ~~is~~ **are** able to break the sticks easily.

The father then ~~tell~~ **tells** his sons, "You are like the sticks. If you are united like the bundle of sticks, you are strong enough to withstand any attacks from enemies. But if there ~~is~~ **are** quarreling and fighting among you, your enemies will be able to defeat you easily." The motto of the United States ~~mean~~ **means** the same thing. The individual states become strong when they are united, but if they try to stand alone, they can be picked off one by one.

Exercise 15-4, p. 287. Pronouns and antecedents: Editing sentences

1.	No one can know if they will get a job in June.	he or she
2.	The growing complexity of economics has not lessened their appeal to students.	its
3.	The teachers' union lost their right to bargain.	its
4.	Anyone who turned in a late paper had their grade reduced.	his or her
5.	Does everybody know where they're going now?	he or she
6.	Neither Herbert nor his brothers could find their book bags.	C
7.	Bettors tend to follow his or her own whims at the racetrack.	their
8.	Every dog on the block barked themselves hoarse that night.	itself
9.	The College of Arts and Sciences changed their entrance requirements.	its
10.	Neither of the two cars is known for their fuel economy.	its
11.	Every police officer anticipated the danger they would face.	he or she
12.	The manager or the employees will get their raises, but not both.	C
13.	No one could see where they were going because of the fog.	he or she (was)
14.	Each of the employees got a raise on his or her anniversary with the company.	C
15.	Someone had left his shoes in my locker.	C
16.	Either Ms. Orosco or Ms. Olsen will receive an award for her teaching.	C
17.	If a person has no pride in their appearance, others can always tell.	his or her
18.	None of the engineers bidding on the contract thought his bid would be too high.	C
19.	Families should install at least one smoke alarm in their homes.	C
20.	Young children, it seems, are just as likely to suffer from stress and anxiety as his or her parents do.	their
21.	The average American receives about 25 credit-card offers per year in their mail.	his or her
22.	The National Highway Traffic Safety Administration estimates that 67 percent of motorcyclists in accidents would not have suffered brain damage if he or she had been wearing a helmet.	they
23.	Scientists say that both length and mass change with their velocity.	C
24.	Each of the speakers wanted to deliver their speech first.	his or her

25. Neither the motorists nor the cyclist seemed to know what they had been thinking when the accident occurred. he or she

26. Every one of the women was married and had brought her children to the seminar. C

27. Neither of the encyclopedias had adequate coverage in its entry on data communication. C

28. The basketball team was celebrating their victory all the way home. its

Exercise 15-5, p. 289. Agreement: Rewriting text

An argument new to our modern age is that of the right to die. One side says that terminally ill people should be allowed to die without having their lives extended with special treatments and equipment. The other side says that dying people should be kept alive by their doctors for as long as possible. In earlier days, before the advent of modern technology, terminally ill people simply died in their beds. Now that life can be extended for weeks and months in a period of protracted dying, we have the problem of how much people should have to say about their own deaths.

In many states, it is legal for people who believe strongly in their right to die to draw up "living wills." With these documents, people can direct physicians not to extend their lives by artificial means—that is, not to use any treatment whose sole purpose is to put off an inevitable death. People draw up these living wills while they are still in good health and of sound mind. And in the states where these documents are legal, physicians will abide by them.

There is still some opposition to such a practice, however. People should be kept alive, so goes the argument, to leave the way open for miraculous recoveries or new treatments or cures. The next step after allowing people to die is to take those people's lives in order to shorten their pain and suffering. Called *euthanasia* or *mercy killing*, this practice is less widely accepted than that of writing living wills, although there are many who say that terminally ill, suffering people should be assisted in their deaths.

The problem is a difficult one that has no easy solution.

Exercise 15-6, p. 291. Agreement: Review

Sample answers:

Verbs—

1. World Wide Web sites and an online service provide access to weather maps and forecasts.
2. Especially when tornadoes or a hurricane is approaching, people flock to sources of weather information.
3. There are available to people in this electronic age many sources of information about the weather.
4. One of the biggest hindrances to getting to and from work locations is the weather.
5. Snow is known to be a common hindrance, as are wind, rain, and ice.

6. A person who spends a great deal of time watching weather on television and computer screen and who reads in the newspapers about the big storms wants to know if weather is becoming more disastrous.

Pronouns—

1. The person who is really hooked on weather forecasting can get the latest satellite images on his or her computer screen.
2. Nearly everyone was watching The Weather Channel on his or her television set during the 1996 blizzard in the eastern United States.
3. Neither most of the major networks nor the Cable News Network could show better ratings on its programs.
4. Meteorologists say that severe storms are normal and no worse than a reasonable person can expect them to be.
5. Neither way of accounting for the occurrence of weather-related disasters can make any person who has lost his or her home feel any better.
6. Nevertheless, people wanting to make themselves feel in better control of the elements turn on their sets or screens.

CHAPTER 16

Adjectives and Adverbs

Exercise 16-1, p. 301. Adjectives and adverbs: Comparing forms

1. adv, *fast*
2. adv, *can hardly*
3. adv, *more*
4. adj, *unique*
5. adj, *better*
6. adj, *faster*
7. adv, *more*
8. adv, *rapidly*
9. adj, *less costly*
10. adv, *first*
11. adj, *bigger*
12. adj, *more attractive*

Exercise 16-2, p. 302. Adjectives and adverbs: Editing forms

1. ~~real~~, really
2. ~~special~~, specially
3. ~~easy~~, easily
7. ~~bad~~, badly
8. ~~most brightest~~, brightest
9. ~~quick~~, quickly
10. ~~never~~, ever
11. ~~near~~, nearly

4. ~~nobody~~, anybody
5. C
6. ~~couldn't~~, could
12. ~~highest~~, higher
13. ~~sudden~~, suddenly
14. ~~serious~~, seriously
15. ~~most unique~~, unique
16. C

Exercise 16-3, p. 303. Articles: Using appropriately

1. an, a
2. the, a
3. the
4. 0
5. a
6. a
7. a, the
8. a, the
9. the, an
10. the, a, a
11. 0, the
12. a, 0
13. a, the
14. a, the

V Clear Sentences

CHAPTER 17

Sentence Fragments

Exercise 17-1, p. 311. Sentence fragments: Revising I

Sample answers:

1. The contrast between the two cats is great. One of them is arrogant, the other highly sociable.
2. C
3. Internet addiction has become a serious matter, one that can interfere with work, school, and relationships.
4. C
5. Chris has one quality that her roommate doesn't have: patience. Chris is so patient that others take advantage of her.
6. Riding the subway, I always read the advertisements above the windows and try to figure out what gimmicks the advertisers use.
7. I tried to be gentle with the old woman. She had insulted me the day before but now needed my help.
8. Perry can be loudmouthed and overbearing, as when he said he should be in a dorm with "better-quality people."
9. The job with a starting salary of $20,000 a year failed to attract qualified applicants even though the advertisement ran for three weeks.
10. Mike seems to be a good father. For example, he takes his children to ball games or on trips or just stays around the house teaching them new games.

Exercise 17-2, p. 313. Sentence fragments: Revising II

Sample answers:

1. The name of the game is knowing the right people, because they'll help you invest your money in the right bank.
2. C
3. It's the last word in typewriters and the very best of its kind.
4. C
5. C
6. It's the best pen you'll ever buy, which is why you should try one today.
7. This gold-plated, roller-ball tip pen is for both men and women.
8. For luxury, beauty, and performance, see your dealer today.
9. Buy Wholefarm Bacon because there is no better bacon.

10. The dependability and efficiency of Toughguy Mowers are worth the price.
11. C
12. Our latest catalog is free. Call now for your copy.
13. If you see the best, then buy what you see.
14. This [pamphlet] is free for the asking. Send for yours today.
15. Are you looking for good music?
16. One of the most nutritious foods is raisins; they're sweet and good.
17. Think cheese, because it's made with real milk.
18. If you buy Northcountry frozen potatoes, you'll find that the taste is in the bag.
19. Take [aspirin] when all you want to do is stop the pain.
20. We are announcing the beginning of a new age.

Exercise 17-3, p. 317. Sentence fragments: Revising III

Sample answers:

1. C
2. Fire extinguishers are devices for putting out small fires, such as those started in waste baskets or mattresses. (Or connect to item 1.)
3. (Connect to item 4.) A fire extinguisher, in addition to a smoke detector, can protect a home from the hazards of fire.
4. C
5. Every day fires break out in 2000 homes in the United States. (Or connect to item 6.)
6. C
7. (Connect to item 6.) Every home should have at least one fire extinguisher, preferably several, and the homeowner or renter should know how to operate each extinguisher.
8. Fire extinguishers are rated by a system of numbers and letters.
9. Higher numbers indicate an extinguisher capable of putting out larger fires. (Or connect to item 8.)
10. The number 9B has a greater capacity than the number 3B. (Or connect to item 9.)
11. (Connect to item 10.) The number 9B has a greater capacity than the number 3B, and 2A has a greater capacity than 1A.
12. C
13. C
14. (Connect to item 13.) B refers to flammable liquid fires, C to fires in electrical equipment.

Exercise 17-4, p. 319. Sentence fragments: Revising text

A. Fragments: 1, 2, 4, 6, 7, 9, 11, 14, 15, 16, 18, 20.

Sample revision:

The Great Barrier Reef stretches for 1200 miles along Australia's northeastern coast. Sometimes called the world's largest living thing, the reef is made up of living coral: purple, green, and pink animals called marine polyps. More than 300 kinds of coral have been identified, each having a scientific name as well as a common name describing its shape, for example mushroom or needle.

In addition to the coral in the Great Barrier Reef, the surrounding sea carries an abundance of other exotic sea life: parrot fish, butterfly fish, sea anemones, and giant clams. Unfortunately, the snorkeled tourist swimming off the sandy beaches may encounter a deadly jellyfish known as the sea wasp, of which there are many, or sharks around the reef. But the sharks, it is said, have never attacked, and with a little care swimmers can avoid the jellyfish. A tour aboard a glass-bottomed cruise boat, including supervised snorkeling in the warm waters around the reef, can be a safe, exhilarating experience, even for a stranger to the waters.

People from North America wanting to visit the Great Barrier Reef should travel to Australia during the northern winter months if they want to experience Australia's summer. Landing in Sydney, they would need to travel north to Cairns, the nearest city to the Great Barrier Reef.

B. Fragments: 3, 4, 7, 8, 10, 11, 13

Sample revision:

Everybody gets itches, because at one time or another all skin itches. Some medical practitioners call itching "the first cousin of pain." It is a message that something is wrong. The itch may be nothing more than dry skin in the winter, but perhaps it is as serious as diabetes or liver disease. So an itch that doesn't go away is a matter of medical concern. One way to avoid itching is to prevent its cause, such as not taking too-hot baths that would dry the skin and avoiding allergens such as pet fur or certain laundry products. Most garden-variety itches go away with a little rubbing, some with the topical application of some kind of ointment such as hydrocortisone. If the itching persists, however, or if it is generalized over the body with no signs of a rash, a person should consult a dermatologist, because the problem may be something requiring medical treatment.

CHAPTER 18

Comma Splices and Fused Sentences

Exercise 18-1, p. 325. Comma splices and fused sentences: Revising

Sample answers:

1. Evidence continues to mount showing that passive smoke causes diseases.
2. C
3. Parents who smoke in the home are putting their children at risk, and roommates endanger nonsmoking partners.
4. Passive smoke is smoke exhaled by the smoker; it is also the smoke emitted from the end of a cigarette.
5. Most of the smoke in a room has not been exhaled by a smoker; rather, it has come from the end of a burning cigarette.
6. When a smoker inhales, his or her lungs remove some of the tar, nicotine, and harmful gases from the tobacco.
7. The smoke from the end of a cigarette is more hazardous because none of the chemicals have been removed.
8. Some of the more dangerous components of smoke are acetylene, benzene, formaldehyde, hydrogen cyanide, nicotine, and propane. They readily enter the bloodstream of smoker and nonsmoker alike.
9. Setting aside a section of a room to separate smokers from nonsmokers is not adequate protection for nonsmokers, because the smoke still circulates in the air.
10. The only way to protect nonsmokers from the harmful effects of smoke is to ban all indoor smoking; therefore, more and more public buildings and workplaces have restrictions.
11. Another problem with smoking tobacco is addiction, which data shows begins in the teen years.
12. This early addiction has long been known by tobacco companies; for that reason they have a history of targeting young teenagers in their advertising.
13. C
14. It is obvious why tobacco companies target teens: they need the business.
15. Many addicted smokers wish they had never started. They were just kids and didn't think they would become addicted.

Exercise 18-2, p. 327. Comma splices and fused sentences: Combining sentences

1. Human cells contain two hundred thousand genes, each controlling specific traits.
2. Mars was named for the Roman god of war because its reddish color was likened to blood spilled in wars.
3. Most diamonds are thought to be very old; in fact, they are among the oldest minerals on earth.

4. Most meteors that enter the earth's atmosphere burn up before striking the ground, but some do not.
5. Time zones are divided by meridians, which run between the north and south poles.
6. Mercury was the Roman god of commerce; curiously, he was also the god of thievery.
7. Reindeer have been domesticated for centuries in Lapland, where they provide meat, milk, clothing, and transportation.
8. Mohandas K. Gandhi gave up a Western way of life and led a life of abstinence and spirituality.
9. Gothic romance novels, which originated with writers such as Mary Shelley and Horace Walpole in the eighteenth and nineteenth centuries, are popular reading today.
10. According to Saint Thomas Aquinas, theology and science cannot contradict one another, nor can there be any conflict between theology and philosophy. **OR** . . . and there cannot be . . .
11. Cheating at school has apparently become more prevalent in recent years, a possible cause being the greater pressure to excel.
12. Soybeans are proven to have a positive effect on health; however, they do have a down side: their taste.
13. Despite a proliferation of Web sites that aid job searches, nine out of ten jobs are still found the old-fashioned way: through ads, job fairs, and recruiters.
14. Although the amount of juvenile crime has decreased since 1994, what we seem to hear about most are the dramatic incidents of crimes by kids.

Exercise 18-3, p. 329. Comma splices and fused sentences: Patterning

No sample answers.

Exercise 18-4, p. 331. Comma splices and fused sentences: Review

Faulty sentences: 1, 2, 6, 7, 11, 12, 13, 16, 17.

Sample revision:

The Country "Down Under"

The landing of 1000 convicts on the shores of what is now Sydney marks what Australians claim was the beginning of their nation, though it was "discovered" by Captain James Cook in 1770. In 1788 the first ship arrived with criminals from the British prisons; they were settled as Australia's first citizens. Since its rough beginning as a British penal colony, Australia has become a country of unique contrasts.

With a national population of about sixteen million, about one million Australians boast convict ancestry. Today about 20 percent of the population is foreign born. Many are Middle Eastern and Asian settlers who have come because of the nation's liberal immigration policies. The original settlers, the aborigines, are in the minority. Numbering about 160,000, they are virtual outcasts in Australia. The country's population is a study in contrasts and diversity.

The land itself provides the greatest contrasts. Geologists say that the continent split off from what we now call South America and Antarctica about sixty million years ago. Its coasts are fertile, but its inland—the outback—is arid; the northeast is tropical rain forest. Off the northeastern coast is the magnificent natural wonder, the Great Barrier Reef, and to the south the Great Bight provides marvelous surfing. Distances are vast between some of the cities, but even more so between settlers in the outback, where people may live as much as two hundred miles apart.

Australia has been known for many years for its characteristic animals. Its koalas, kangaroos, wallabies, and platypuses live nowhere else in the world except in captivity. Even though kangaroos are the national symbol, every year millions are slaughtered as farmers try to prevent them from destroying crops.

Americans know about Australia from the *Crocodile Dundee* movies, from the novel and television miniseries *The Thornbirds*, and from popular entertainers. These and other entertainment give us a glimpse of the world "down under." We can learn more if we want to, because Australia is definitely in the news.

CHAPTER 19

Pronoun Reference

Exercise 19-1, p. 339. Pronoun reference: Revising sentences

Sentences are sample answers:

1. their, they, they
   Gerardo and Maria checked their bags at the ticket counter, but then they weren't sure if the bags were safe.
2. It
   One of the US Justice Department's initiatives is to educate kids on "cyberethics." The initiative has evolved from numerous hacking-related investigations.
3. you, your, your, your
   For people who lived in the nineteenth century, their feet and their horses were their only private means of transportation.
4. their, They
   In a recent study, nearly three-fourths of job-seekers admitted lying on their resumes, such as omitting past jobs and altering education facts.
5. their
   Some critics charge that school districts have spent millions of dollars to install computers, yet the potential of those computers is not being met.
6. which, my
   The exam was scheduled for Tuesday, and testing then was not in my plans.
7. their
   In some cities, children encourage friends, neighbors, and relatives in ~~their~~ recycling efforts.
8. we, it, it
   After discussing the repair for the car, we knew it was time the damage was taken care of.
9. their
   On the Internet, a student can access data, resources, and experts in his or her area of interest.
10. that, this
    People who serve on established committees and want more business could use the results of this survey.
11. They
    People say that trouble comes in threes.
12. they, them
    Fears are normal in childhood, but how children overcome their fears differs from child to child.
13. she
    In her groundbreaking novel *The Women's Room*, Marilyn French questions accepted norms regarding women's roles.

14. This
Medical researchers have discovered a new medication that may reduce deaths from strokes and heart attacks.

Exercise 19-2, p. 341. Pronoun reference: Replacing vague pronouns

Sample answer:

Harriet likes to anthropomorphize. This tendency means she attributes human characteristics to animals. She anthropomorphizes birds, squirrels, deer, raccoons, and any other living thing that happens to pass her way. She especially attributes human characteristics to cats, of which she has two.

Harriet thinks that squirrels eat her petunias just to upset her, whereas they probably eat them because they like the way petunias taste. Squirrels probably also have their squirrel reasons for digging up the lawn and dropping acorn scraps on Harriet's patio, reasons which only faintly resemble human motivations. That difference is probably true of the deer and the raccoons too. They probably enjoy the corn she sets out in the yard, but as they stand there munching that corn they probably don't give the slightest thought to how it got there or who put it there. In fact, if they saw her coming around the corner of the house, they would quickly disappear.

The situation is different with Harriet's cats. They don't run away; instead they hang around and expect Harriet to care for them. At least she sees the situation that way. Maybe they're not actually grateful, she thinks, but they do expect her care. And when she talks to them, she says they respond with reasoned answers, a position that has to be an extreme case of anthropomorphism. When she asks if they're hungry, they of course answer "M-yah." When she left them out in the rain one day they scolded her severely in answer to her question if they were wet. Well, anyone who knows cats would agree that they probably were indeed annoyed about her neglect.

But Harriet really does take anthropomorphism too far. Animals do think and feel, but that fact does not mean they're like people.

Exercise 19-3, p. 343. Pronoun Reference: Combining sentences

Sample answers:

Lennie, Annie, and Gus were students at Riverland Community College. Because they were nontraditional students, they took some of their courses through the office of continuing studies. As students who took some of these courses, they would not meet in classrooms; instead, they did all the work at home. The courses were called "self-paced."

Lennie, Annie, and Gus liked doing self-paced courses, because they could adjust their work schedules more easily and could work around their other courses. But there were things they didn't like about the self-paced courses too. One was that they missed the interactions with other students in the classroom. Another was the specter of procrastination. Lennie, Annie, and Gus had never prided themselves on their self-discipline. Now that they had no deadlines for getting their assignments done, it seemed that they were always having to remind themselves about doing them. They could take "incompletes" at the end of the term, but doing so didn't solve their problems. The only difference was that now the problems had carried over into the next term.

They decided they really must do something about disciplining themselves.

Exercise 19-4, p. 344. Pronoun reference: Review

Sample answer:

Before 1889 the little town of Westin had no lumberyard where its citizens could buy lumber. Lumber was available only at the sawmills, and they didn't sell it to the general public. This situation was a problem for people who wanted to build their own house or to add a room or a porch. But it was an opportunity for an enterprising businessman. William Rand, who had just migrated from Germany with his family, was such a person He was a skilled carpenter, and he knew wood. But William didn't have any money, and that deficiency was a problem.

He discussed his idea with the owner of one of the sawmills in the area around Westin, and the owner agreed that it was a good plan. They decided to go into business together and start a lumberyard in downtown Westin. So, with the sawmill owner putting up the money and Rand running the business, they opened their lumber yard with five loads of unsorted lumber that they got from the mill as initial stock.

Today the business is still owned by the Rand family, but it's his grandsons now who are in charge of it. And the citizens of Westin can still buy their lumber there.

CHAPTER 20

Shifts

Exercise 20-1, p. 349. Shifts in person and number: Revising sentences for consistency

Sample answer:

22. Have you ever heard of the blue-footed booby? It's a bird that lives off the west coast of Mexico.
23. An ardent bird watcher could also see these birds on the Galapagos Islands, where the birder might see the boobies diving for fish.
24. The birds are about 30 inches long, about the size of geese, and they actually have blue feet.
25. Blue-footed boobies have brown and white plumage that contrasts with their bright blue feet.
26. The major food of the boobies is fish, which they catch in spectacular dives into the water.
27. C
28. This bird is called "booby,"a Spanish word meaning "stupid fellow," because of its clumsiness on land.

Exercise 20-2, p. 350. Shifts in tense: Revising sentences for consistency

27. Some of the students who are in college today attended one-room schools.
28. These were schools where grades one through eight had class in the same room.
29. The schools, in fact, had only one room, so all the grades studied together.
30. Then, of course, there was only teacher, who instructed students at all levels.
31. That single teacher also taught reading, arithmetic, writing, history, and everything else the children had to learn.
32. C
33. They remember also that the various age groups got along well together despite their age differences.
34. C

Exercise 20-3, p. 351. Shifts: Revising sentences for consistency

Sample answers:

1. He said he bought the recorder without asking whether it worked.
2. You should stay clear of credit cards because they encourage you to spend more money than you have.
3. To have it printed, take it to the shop on Wednesday, and then call the next day.
4. Although the poet's words are fascinating, I do not know what they mean.

5. She wanted to buy flannel, but she learned that she was allergic to it.
6. If one wants to get the most from college, one must work hard, ask questions, and keep an open mind. *or*
To get the most from college, you must work hard, ask questions, and keep an open mind.
7. The two countries had had peaceful relations for a decade when suddenly a border dispute erupted into a war.
8. He said my face was red and asked whether I was embarrassed.
He said, "Your face is red. Are you embarrassed?"
9. People who receive repeated nuisance phone calls have no choice but to change their numbers.
10. After a mugger attacked the elderly woman, the police took her to the hospital.
11. You should be aware that poor night vision can endanger your life.
12. The characters in the movie are average people, but they have more than average problems.

Exercise 20-4, p. 353. Shifts: Review

Our trip to the beach got off to a bad start when the car
had **We**
has two flat tires a mile from home. You can always count on
some trouble with our car but usually nothing this annoying.
the manager had not canceled our
We arrived at the motel late, but fortunately our reservations
reservations **because he remembered**
had not been canceled by the manager, who remembers us from
we would
the last time we vacationed there. He asked how long would we
whether we wanted
be staying and did we want the seafood special for dinner. We
unpacked our luggage.
checked into our room and our luggage was unpacked. Everything
was going smoothly. Then we went to dinner and turned in for
We
the night. One would have expected that the rest of the
we
vacation should be routine if not fun. But that night each
all **got** **our**
one of us gets sick from their seafood dinner. The next
morning the rain came, and for three days we just sat in the
to make our trip home.
room playing cards until it was time that our trip home could
to be made.

CHAPTER 21

Misplaced and Dangling Modifiers

Exercise 21-1, p. 361. Misplaced modifiers: Revising sentences

Sentences are sample revisions:

1. as a lifestyle
   Many people have chosen vegetarianism as a lifestyle.
2. all
   They feel that all eating of animal meat is wrong.
3. often
   Often people who see immorality in eating meat become vegetarians.
4. just
   Some vegetarians eat just plant products.
5. for maintaining nutrition and their sense of morality
   For maintaining nutrition and their sense of morality, they limit their diet to grains, legumes, vegetables, fruits, nuts, and seeds.
6. only
   Others supplement their diet only with dairy products such as cheese and milk.
7. in addition to plants and milk products
   Still others eat eggs in addition to plants and milk products.
8. in order to have adequate protein in the diet
   In order to have adequate protein in the diet, it is not necessary to eat meat.
9. C
10. if they were to consider the source of their meat
    A vegetarian feels that carnivores would have less of an appetite for their meat if they were to consider its source.
11. C
12. today
    Today meat comes packaged and ready for cooking.
13. some day
    Vegetarians say that a trip some day to a slaughterhouse might cure carnivores of their taste for meat.
14. C
15. at an alarming rate
    At an alarming rate, South American rain forests are destroyed so that more cattle can be raised to supply beef for North American fast-food restaurants.

Exercise 21-2, p. 363. Adjectives and adverbs: Arranging appropriately

1. the twisted old oak tree

2. some modern Hindu religious laws
3. any moderately functional electric toaster
4. the week-old daily newspaper
5. a thick hot ham sandwich
6. one long forgotten, disgustingly overripe banana
7. a pair of new red patent leather shoes
8. a worn-out black felt-tip pen
9. the fourteen-year-old yellow convertible car
10. some recently released computer software
11. two extra-large gray silk shirts

Exercise 21-3, p. 364. Misplaced and dangling modifiers: Revising text

Sample answer:

Not wanting to be known for their lack of discrimination, some serious readers shun mystery novels. These readers believe that all mystery novels are formulaic and unperceptive. People who avidly read books in this genre will agree that many mystery novels are indeed empty of real substance. As prolific readers, they can name particular authors and particular books that fit the description. Apparently these books are quickly written with insufficient editing, so that careful readers find dangling modifiers, subject-verb disagreement, unclear pronoun reference, and so on. Worse yet, the plots and motivations lack credibility, and the characters are flat and one-dimensional. But this description fits only part of the books in this genre. Some authors who specialize in mystery novels care diligently about their craft and view their mystery writing seriously and professionally. To learn which writers are careful and which ones are only in a hurry to get the next blockbuster on the market, readers must do a lot of reading.

Exercise 21-4, p. 365. Dangling modifiers: Revising sentences

Sample answers:

1. When you are reading poetry, rhythm often contributes to meaning.
2. After buying a new pair of boots, you should treat them with a protective finish. *or*
   After buying a new pair of boots, a consumer should treat them with a protective finish.
3. The vet recommended that we leave our puppy overnight so it could recover from the surgery.
4. When painting the walls, you should take care to protect the floor from dripping brushes.
5. After adding three cups of ground chickpeas, heat the pot.
6. Taking a look at the gifts, the child selected the smallest box.
7. C
8. Being a nonconformist, she chose to wear a multicolored wig.
9. With no concern that the audience was bored, Carson continued to lecture for two hours.
10. To get the employer's attention, you should send an attractive and informative rsum.
11. To get the costumes done in time for tonight's taping, we need help in the costume department.
12. When Davidson entered the game, we all cheered him as the best player on the team.
13. Having been told the qualifications for jurors and then shown a videotape, the jurors broke for lunch.
14. When entering the building, have your identification card in clear view.
15. Since I broke my ankle, my brother has been driving me to school.

CHAPTER 22

Mixed and Incomplete Sentences

Exercise 22-1, p. 371. Mixed sentences: Revising

Sample answers:

1. She made the clerk angry when she bargained for a discount.
2. Just because you took a course in computer programming, you're not an expert.
3. You lose your chance when you hesitate.
4. Someone who knows that fighting and sports are not necessarily related could be very disturbed at a hockey game.
5. The fire that burned down the hardware store on First Street was caused by an arsonist.
6. He was lonely because he had a quick, violent temper.
7. Having a college education means that you have more skills for the job market and a better knowledge of the world.
8. Revising my resume has improved my chances of a job interview.
9. Psychology is the study of behavioral characteristics.
10. Good oral communication skills can make you a more attractive candidate for the job.
11. The meeting starts at 6:15.
12. Sending your order now qualifies you for a special gift.
13. I missed class because the bus was late.
14. On the way to the train, I fell and broke my ankle.

Exercise 22-2, p. 373. Incomplete sentences: Revising

Changed elements are underlined.

1. We suspect that Judy is more devoted to music than <u>she is to</u> Andy. *or*
   We suspect that Judy is more devoted to music than Andy <u>is</u>.
2. The administration claims to believe <u>in</u> and plan for the college's future.
3. Some brands of vodka contain more alcohol than any <u>other</u> beverage.
4. I was going seventy miles an hour and <u>was</u> stopped for speeding.
5. The Hilton's room service is as good as the Astor<u>'s</u>.
6. They were fond <u>of</u> and totally devoted to their grandchild.
7. The second-night audience found the play more impressive than the opening-night audience <u>did</u>.
8. This sandwich is as good <u>as</u>, if not better than, the ones my mother makes.
9. Thank you for your support.
10. Faulkner's novels are more complex than any <u>other</u> author's.
11. The audience saw <u>that</u> the musician on the podium was unable to proceed.
12. Fruit juice stains are harder to remove than grass <u>stains</u>.

13. I came to realize that some points in the article are true.

14. All those opposed to or in favor of the resolution raised their hands.

Exercise 22-3, p. 375 Mixed and incomplete sentences: Review

Sample answer:

~~During~~ My first day at college was somewhat frightening for me. As a student who is older than many others, I was unsure of my ability to do as well as if not better than the younger students fresh out high school. I knew I had brains, but I felt a little rusty because it had been fifteen years since I graduated from high school. Also, I had a family that still expected me to cook most of their meals, see that they had clean clothes, and tuck them into bed at night. My going back to school was all right with them as long as it didn't inconvenience them too much.

So there I was, on campus my first day. I had already undergone the horrors of registering for classes and now was faced with finding the classrooms, enduring the pandemonium of the bookstore, and memorizing the bus schedule to make sure I got to class on time and home before my kids did.

~~By~~ Sitting in class was the easy part. The instructors seemed very open, friendly, and knowledgeable, and the assignments, I thought, were manageable. The biggest surprise was the other students. They were less actively involved in the classes than I was, and their questions didn't seem any more intelligent than mine. I learned that they have outside jobs that take time comparable to that of my housework and that many of them had, like me, been out of high school for a few years.

So I ended that frightening first day feeling confident in my ability to manage college work and my home responsibilities.

Exercise 22-4, p. 377. Omissions and faulty repetitions: Revising text

```
  There
  ^ were two major earthquakes in Mexico City in 1985.  The
two quakes they happened on September 19 and 20. They measured
8.1 and 7.3 on the Richter scale.  The powerful earthquakes
                                                      of
killed more than 7000 people and damaged thousands ^ buildings.
It                                                       there
^ was a bad time for the people of that city.  Afterwards, ^
was rubble all over the city.

  Some scientists think the reason for the intensity of the
quakes it was the underlying geological formations of the
```

(In the passage above, "they" in line 2 and "it" in the last line are struck through.)

is

region. Mexico City ^ built on an ancient lake bed and bog, making it shake like Jell-O in an earthquake. Another reason

is

^ that the city is near the boundary of two tectonic plates. These tectonic plates, which make up the earth's crust, ~~they~~ collided, and one slipped under the other, causing the quake.

was

The center of the quake ^ 224 miles from Mexico City.

There

^ was another serious earthquake in Mexico City only 27 years earlier. ~~Was~~ In 1957 ~~that~~ extensive damage occurred.

the

Many of ^ places that were destroyed ~~they~~ were never rebuilt.

CHAPTER 23

Emphasizing Ideas

Exercise 23-1, p. 383. Emphasis: Revising sentences

Sample answers:

1. The foundation will award the prize for the first time in fifty years.
2. Legal gambling can increase tax revenues and tourism. It can also increase crime.
3. With appliances that can be heated to 500 degrees and poisons that can kill instantly, the kitchen is a room filled with perils.
4. He had only six dollars left for cat food, for his dinner, and for his heart medicine.
5. Shank scored the winning point.
6. Carrying its prey in its beak, the hawk swooped upward, flapping its wings.
7. Afraid of theft, the guard placed a lock on the warehouse door. *or*
   The guard placed a lock on the warehouse door because he was afraid of theft.
8. Because of the steady downpour, the players ruined their uniforms, they could not hold on to the ball, and three of them tore ligaments.
9. In a monotonous voice the speaker discussed nutrition for three hours.
10. Management will likely withhold raises this year.

Exercise 23-2, p. 385. Emphasis: Combining sentences

Sample answers:

1. When the largest bank cut its lending rate, the other large banks followed. The experts thought the rates would keep dropping, but the rates held steady.
2. I receive calls for wrong numbers during rainstorms. One rainy afternoon when I was trying to study, I got twenty-seven calls for an ice-cream shop.
3. Summer jobs were hard to find in town: no businesses were hiring, there was no construction work, and the gas stations were going broke.
4. Police officers need special habits and driving skills. They must keep their car keys handy, must always remember to park facing an exit, and must drive cautiously at high speed.
5. The white-haired, wrinkled old woman looked innocent. Her blue eyes even twinkled as she pulled a revolver and took my wallet.
6. A visit to a nursing home does not have to be depressing. One can cheer up the residents by bringing along a small child and by taking time to smile and say hello.
7. *Breakout* by Ron LeFlore, my favorite biography, is an inspiring story about how LeFlore lived in prison and how he used his skill at baseball to rejoin society.

8. When the tanker truck overturned, gasoline spread across the highway and ignited a field. The resulting fire killed twelve head of cattle.
9. The old and tattered magazine described Leon Spinks, who could have been a champion for several years but who seemed to lose faith in himself.
10. Because they shed very little, are obedient, and are gentle with children, dachshunds make great pets.

CHAPTER 24

Using Coordination and Subordination

Exercise 24-1, p. 393. Coordination: Combining sentences

Sample answers:

1. The human eye can distinguish about 10 million colors, yet we have names for only a few.
2. A friend may tell you that his new car is blue, but the blue you imagine may not be the blue of his car.
3. The cells in the eye that distinguish colors function only in light, so in dim light we see only tones of gray.
4. The cells that perceive colors are called *cones,* and those that perceive black and white are called *rods.*
5. Rods function better than cones in semidarkness, for they are sensitive to movement in dim light.
6. People who are color-blind may have some nonfunctioning cones, for they cannot see particular colors.
7. You can call red, blue, and yellow the primary colors, or you might designate the primaries as red, blue, and green.
8. The eye is quite adept at distinguishing fine differences in color, yet sometimes the eye makes mistakes.
9. After looking at something dark, you see a light image when you look away, and after looking at a color, such as green, you see its opposite, such as red.
10. This type of mistake is called *successive contrast*, and it's a normal part of vision.

Exercise 24-2, p. 395. Subordination: Combining sentences

Sample answers:

1. Although his shoulders are slightly stooped, he still looks energetic.
2. Tonight he played his greatest role: Lothario.
3. Nearly at the end of our trip, we were stopped by the state police.
4. After the meeting ended, the hall was again deserted.
5. Unwelcome pests, sparrows may eat as much as 6 percent of a grain crop.
6. Because she wore jogging shoes, the waiter refused to seat her.
7. Recovering, the patient was depressed and irritable.
8. Feeling embarrassed, he could not get a word out.
9. Although German stereo components are often of high quality, they are usually more expensive than Japanese components. *or*
   Although German stereo components are usually more expensive than Japanese components, they are often of high quality.
10. I did not know how to interpret the question because it had four possible answers.

Exercise 24-3, p. 397. Coordination and subordination: Revising text

Sample answers:

1. A good example of corruption occurred recently in the US Navy. According to a Washington columnist, an officer was demoted for reporting some of his fellow officers. The officers, who were responsible for training recruits, had sold the recruits uniforms that were supposed to be issued free.
2. A triangle, tattooed on the back of his hand when he was sixteen, symbolized the brass triangle he had played in a rock band.
3. The night was black, and the road was slippery. The car ran up an embankment and rolled over twice, causing the occupants to be thrown out. Even though no one was injured, the car was a total loss.
4. The first Earth Day, held on April 22, 1970, is said to have initiated the environmental movement in the United States. With the participation of about 20 million Americans, it was the largest organized demonstration to that date. Local demonstrations involved nature walks and direct action against polluters. In New York City, an eco-fair attended by 100,000 people was held in Union Square. When the US Congress formally adjourned for the day, its members were able to attend teach-ins in their districts. Because of Earth Day, people have increased awareness of the need to stop polluting and begin recycling; a far-reaching effect was the creation of the Environmental Protection Agency in 1971.
5. Wyatt Berry Stapp Earp, lawman and gunfighter in the American frontier, was born in 1848 in Monmouth, Illinois. After first serving as a policeman in Kansas, he later moved to Tombstone, Arizona, where in 1881 he participated in the infamous gunfight at the O.K. Corral. He obviously survived the gunfight, because records show that he died much later, in 1929.

CHAPTER 25

Using Parallelism

Exercise 25-1, p. 403. Parallelism: Writing sentences

New sentences will vary.

1. Brazil is bordered by Venezuela, Guyana, Suriname, and French Guiana.
2. Brazil is a federation of 22 states, four territories, and the federal district of Brasilia.
3. The official language is Portuguese, but the population is an amalgam.
4. Brazil's economy depends heavily not only on agriculture but on its mineral resources as well.
5. Occupying nearly half of the continent and having a varied topography, Brazil is the largest country in South America.
6. Rio de Janeiro is Brazil's second-largest city and its former capital.
7. Tourists flock to Rio to attend its pre-Lenten carnival and to take in its natural setting.
8. Brasilia, one of the world's newest cities and the capital of Brazil since 1960, is situated in the sparsely settled interior.
9. The largest city in Brazil is Sao Paulo: Brazil's commercial, financial, and industrial center.
10. The Amazon River traverses through northern Brazil and into the Atlantic Ocean.

Exercise 25-2, p. 405. Parallelism: Combining sentences

Sample answers:

1. The history of English has been divided into three stages: Old English, Middle English, and Modern English.
2. Old English ran from about 600 to about 1100, Middle English from 1100 to about 1500, and Modern English from about 1500 to the present.
3. These dates mean that *Beowulf* was written in the Old English period, that Chaucer wrote *Canterbury Tales* during the Middle English period, and that Shakespeare wrote during the Modern period.
4. The Modern period is sometimes divided into Early Modern, ending in 1700, and Late Modern, beginning in 1700 and continuing to the present.
5. English has its roots in the language of three Germanic tribes—the Angles, the Saxons, and the Jutes—commonly called Anglo-Saxons.
6. Some of the most common words in use today have their origin in Anglo-Saxon, or Old English—for example, *the, man, mother,* and *and.*
7. Middle English dates from the Norman Conquest of England in 1066 and was strongly influenced by the French-speaking Normans.

8. Thousands of French words entered the English vocabulary during this period, many of them among our most common: *beef, music, nice,* and *flower.*
9. Modern English is characterized by changes in pronunciation; *sea,* for example, once rhymed with *hay,* and *moon* once rhymed with *loan.*
10. These changes in pronunciation and the invention of the printing press in 1475 contributed toward apparent inconsistencies in spelling today.

Exercise 25-3, p. 407. Parallelism: Editing text

Changed elements are underlined. Sample revision:

The birthplace of Martin Luther King, Jr., in Atlanta, Georgia, is a national historic site run by the National Park Service. Located at 501 Auburn Avenue in the Atlanta neighborhood known as Sweet Auburn, the King house is a tourist attraction made up of both two- and three- story Victorian houses owned by black professional people and the row houses of the black poor.

The house where King grew up is a Queen Anne frame building with two stories and a large front porch. The historic structure, painted white with dark shutters at the windows, gives testimony of the civil rights leader's boyhood. The lower floor has a front parlor with a piano and other original furniture. There the King children would play games like Monopoly and Old Maid after they had finished their chores—stoking the furnace or brushing crumbs from the dinner table. In the kitchen are a 1930s-style icebox, a black stove, and a big kitchen cabinet. Visitors can imagine King's mother, Alberta, preparing the family meals here while the children played on the green linoleum floor. Upstairs are the bedrooms. In the big bedroom that belonged to the parents, all the King children were born.

One block to the west is the Center for Non-Violent Social Change, directed by Coretta Scott King, Martin Luther King's widow. The Center houses a museum that informs visitors about King's adult life and is open to the public. Visitors to this museum can see both personal items and public mementos. One historical item is a replica of King's Nobel Peace Prize, awarded in 1964. A touching personal memento is the key to the door of the hotel room where he was staying the day he was assassinated, and another is the wallet he had with him on that day.

April 4, 1969, the day King was shot in Memphis, Tennessee, is a day of infamy. But King will long be remembered as the foremost champion of civil rights and the upholder of peace and brotherhood.

Atlanta tourists can visit one of these buildings or both of them. Admission to both is free, and visitors can take free guided walking tours of the Sweet Auburn district as well.

CHAPTER 26

Achieving Variety

Exercise 26-1, p. 413. Sentence beginnings: Revising for variation

Sample answers:

1. Penicillin can cure her disease. Unfortunately, she is allergic to penicillin.
2. Although the bamboo basket looks frail, it is really quite sturdy.
3. Because the speech was priced at one dollar a copy, not one copy was sold.
4. Falling five stories to the street, the crane smashed a truck.
5. The party invitations omitted the address. Consequently, just a few people came.
6. Even though he never became a great architect, he was not obscure.
7. Sinking a shot from thirty feet, Johnson won the game.
8. There is money in the budget for travel.
9. Being a good photographer certainly requires skill. In addition, it requires money.
10. Swimming in the pond, we heard a shot from across the meadows.

Exercise 26-2, p. 415. Varying sentences in paragraphs

Sample answers:

1. Although almost everyone is afraid of something, some people are so paralyzed by multiple phobias that they cannot leave the house for fear of an emotional collapse. Treating such people is a slow process, for they have to become comfortable with each feared object or situation. The treatment, which may occur in a laboratory or in natural surroundings, eliminates the phobias one at a time. At the end of the treatment, the patient can often resume a normal life.

2. Some business executives are concerned about the quality of education in the public schools and whether students are learning English, math, science, social studies, and communications. These executives are concerned that in the future they will have to hire illiterate workers who will not be able to keep pace with changes in industry. Workers who cannot read well affect productivity and efficiency. As a result, the businesses teach basic skills: grammar, typing, and spelling. But the executives are not happy with the present state of affairs, thinking that uniform testing may be an answer.

3. Some business leaders recommend uniform testing, thinking that it may improve the quality of education. The tests, they say, should be uniform for each state, as well as comprehensive and reliable. Given to all schoolchildren, the tests would make the schools more accountable to the public, and they would tell taxpayers—who support the public schools—how well students are learning. Accountability is important, but substantive, informed changes are important too, as many business leaders and educators know.

VII PUNCTUATION

CHAPTER 27

End Punctuation

Exercise 27-1, p. 419. End punctuation: Editing sentences

1. dog!"
2. C
3. cabinet.
4. C
5. Never?"
6. Kid?"
7. exercise.
8. Dr. Baer
9. be.
10. reading.
11. arrive?"
12. again.
13. January.
14. yet.
15. C
16. out!"
17. videotape.
18. out!" yelled
19. Rev. Winters
20. late?" she
21. DC.
22. CARE
23. Greenland.
24. C
25. money.
26. MA or M.A.
27. C
28. C
29. 10:00 p.m.
30. St. John's, St. Olaf

CHAPTER 28

The Comma

Exercise 28-1, p. 437. Commas between main clauses and after introductory elements: Revising text

1. Discovering the origin of English is like reading a detective story. Applying deductive reasoning to available clues, linguists have traced its beginnings to a hypothetical language called Indo-European. This language did actually exist, but there is no record of it other than in the languages that derived from it. In addition to English, among these languages existing today are German, Swedish, French, Greek, and Russian. To discover similar roots, linguists traced common words. For example *night* in English is *nacht* in German, *natt* in Swedish, *nuit* in French, *nuktos* in Greek, and *noch* in Russian. Interestingly, some of these languages that derive from Indo-European are classified as Romance, or Latinate, and some are Germanic. Still others have other histories.

2. On the basis of the presence or absence of certain words in the related languages, linguists speculate that Indo-European existed in Eastern Europe several thousand years before Christ. They found evidence of words for *bear* and *snow,* but they discovered no common words for *camel* and *ocean.* Using this evidence, they supposed that the language was spoken by an inland people that experienced winter climates.

3. At some point, Indo-European split into Eastern and Western Branches, and these branches then divided again. Like English, Swedish derived from a branch of Western Indo-European, the Germanic. Greek and French also derived from a branch of Western Indo-European, but Russia's origins are in Eastern Indo-European.

Exercise 28-2, p. 439. Commas in sentences with nonessential elements, absolute phrases, and phrases of contrast: Editing

Added commas are underlined.

1. The trial, which lasted for three days, ended with a verdict of guilty.
2. C
3. C
4. All the banks, I hear, refuse to lend money to international students.
5. Two men, one of them wearing a ski mask, robbed the small grocery store where I work.
6. C
7. We are, after all, here to get an education.
8. There were few surprises, I thought, in last night's game.
9. Senator Cuomo, who chairs the finance committee, voted against tax reform.
10. Her health failing, Sarah called her children around her.

11. The audience becoming impatient,_ the theater manager asked for a little more time to get the sound system working.
12. My dog,_ whose name is Jasper,_ eats two rawhide bones a day.
13. The tax forms,_ six pages of figures,_ were mailed yesterday.
14. The delay,_ during which the pitcher's arm tightened up,_ lasted an hour.
15. C
16. I replied, "Yes,_ I would like to play music professionally."
17. Every morning I drink grapefruit juice,_ which contains vitamins,_ and eat a brownie,_ which tastes good.
18. Hypnotism,_ still not allowable in court testimony,_ is a fertile method for developing one's memory.
19. The songs of birds,_ for instance, are more complex than they sound.
20. The music blaring next door,_ I was unable to concentrate on my reading.

Exercise 28-3, p. 441 Commas with nonessential elements, absolute phrases, and phrases of contrast: Combining sentences

Sample answers:

A.

1. The Wortham Theater Center, built over a six-year period, now houses Houston's Grand Opera and the Houston Ballet.
2. No public money was used to build the Wortham, which cost $72 million.
3. The building was given to the city of Houston, which now operates it together with the Opera and the Ballet.
4. Its lobby, one of the largest in America, is huge.
5. The Wortham, like other postmodern architecture, is so big that it makes people feel small.
6. The Wortham covers two city blocks, its exterior being brown Texas brick, rose-colored granite, and glass.
7. Inside the lobby are eight large steel sculptures, which seem almost too small for this huge lobby.
8. The Wortham has two theaters and five large rehearsal halls, all of which are contained in one of the city blocks.
9. The Brown Theater, seating 1176, is the opera house.
10. The Roy Cullen Theater is smaller, seating 1100.

B.

1. The Ganges is named for the goddess Ganga, the Indians believing that she frees their souls.
2. The Ganges is heavily polluted, upstream industries and urban sewage having dirtied it.
3. Many people come to the river to die, one of its major pollutants being the ashes and bones of cremated bodies.
4. With its waters carrying many diseases, thousands of devout Hindus bathe in the Ganges every day.
5. Its health standards in conflict with religion, the Indian government wants to clean up the river.
6. Part of the plan is to build sewers and treatment facilities, waste water to be processed there.
7. About 75 percent of Ganges pollution coming from waste water, the treatment facilities would make a big difference.

8. The government also proposes to build large electric crematories, this move being more controversial than that of waste treatment facilities.
9. The old wooden crematories would be replaced by the new ones, the old crematories' waste and ash greatly polluting the river.
10. The government also proposes to build public laundries, detergents from people doing their laundry in the river thus being contained and treated.

C.

1. Aristotle, not Plato, wrote *The Art of Rhetoric*.
2. Aristotle describes a rhetoric of persuasion, or one of exposition.
3. Aristotle, unlike some politicians today, felt that rhetoric had noble aims.
4. For Aristotle, rhetoric was a means of uplifting an audience, never a means of insulting them.
5. But rhetoric could be used to evoke negative emotions like anger, not just positive ones like honor.

Exercise 28-4, p. 445 Commas with series, coordinate adjectives, dates, addresses, long numbers, and quotations: Editing

Added commas are underlined.

1. A high-priced,_ skimpy meal was all that was available.
2. After testing 33,_107 subjects, the scientist still thought she needed a bigger sample.
3. C
4. "I need fifty volunteers, now,_" the physical education teacher said ominously.
5. The shop is located at 2110 Greenwood Street,_ Kennett Square,_ Pennsylvania 19348.
6. The open mine attracted children looking for adventure,_ couples needing privacy,_ and old drunks seeking a place to sleep.
7. The area around Riverside,_ California,_ has some of the most polluted air in the country.
8. The records disappeared from the doctor's office in Olean,_ New York,_ yesterday.
9. Seven lonely,_ desperate people come to the neighborhood center for counseling every night.
10. The lantern has a large,_ very heavy base.
11. The town council designated the area's oldest,_ largest house as a landmark.
12. C
13. The office is located at 714 W. Lincoln,_ Harlingen,_ Texas.
14. The November 17,_ 1944,_ issue of the *Times* carried the submarine story.
15. The team lost its final games by the scores 72-66,_ 72-68,_ and 72-70.

Exercise 28-5, p. 446. Misused and overused commas: Editing

Commas that do not belong are circled.

1. Legal residents of the United States can enter Canada, without a passport.
2. Visitors to Canada, who do not have US citizenship, must have a valid passport.
3. US citizens who want to enter Canada, should carry some identification.
4. This identification might be, a birth certificate, a baptismal certificate, or a voter's certificate.
5. C
6. People taking pet dogs and cats across the border, must have a certificate showing that the animals have recently been vaccinated against rabies.
7. However, puppies and kittens under three months of age are not restricted.

8. Seeing-eye dogs also, are not required to have certification.
9. People who want to take other kinds of pets with them, such as, turtles and parrots, should check requirements.
10. Visitors to Canada should also know, that there are restrictions on plants.
11. C
12. Merchandise over certain limits, is subject to customs duty.
13. US residents who have been in Canada for 48 hours, or less, can bring back $25 worth of certain restricted merchandise.
14. This merchandise includes, perfume, 4 ounces of alcoholic beverages, 10 cigars, and 50 cigarettes.
15. US residents, who have been in Canada for more than 48 hours, may bring up to $400 back with them.
16. Restricted merchandise such as alcohol and tobacco, has limits.
17. C
18. Tourists who want to bring plants home with them should ask, what these restrictions are.
19. They could also learn that, "bringing whalebone and sealskin into the United States is illegal."
20. C

Exercise 28-6, p. 447. Commas: Editing text

Added commas are underlined; unneeded commas are slashed.

Argentina, the second largest country in South America, extends 2300 miles from north to south. It is about one-third the size of the United States, not counting Alaska and Hawaii. The land was settled by people from many European countries, but/most of the Argentines are descendants of early Spanish settlers/and Spanish and Italian immigrants. The official language of the nation is Spanish. The Argentine people, most of whom live in the cities, are generally better educated than people in other South American countries. About 90 percent can read and write. Some Argentines live in large, modern apartment buildings, and others live in Spanish- style buildings with adobe walls, tile roofs, and wrought-iron grillwork on the windows. The homes of the poorer people, of course, are not so grand.

Argentina is a major producer of cattle, sheep, wool, and grain. On the pampa, which is a fertile grassy area covering about a fifth of the country, cowboys, called *gauchos,* tend large herds of cattle, and farmers raise sheep, hogs, and wheat. Farther south, in the windswept region of Patagonia, people raise sheep/and pump oil. Because the country has such a wide range of elevation/and distance from the equator, it has a climate/that varies greatly. For example, the north has heavy rainfall, the central area has moderate precipitation, and parts of Patagonia are desert. Being in the Southern Hemisphere, Argentina has seasons just the opposite of those in North America, the hottest days occurring in January and February and the coldest in July and August.

Since its first settlement in the 1500s, when early explorers hoped to find silver in the land, Argentina has found/that its real wealth is in its fertile soil and its lively people.

CHAPTER 29

The Semicolon

Exercise 29-1, p. 453. Semicolon: Editing sentences

Added punctuation is underlined; unneeded punctuation is slashed.

1. A 1915 cookbook predicts, "The fireless cooker will become recognized as one of the greatest achievements of the century."
2. "No home should be without one," it said; "every cook should use one."
3. Its primary advantages were that it saved fuel and prevented burning and scorching; it also kept cooking odors from spreading throughout the house.
4. The fireless cooker was little more than an insulated box working on the principle that wood is a poor conductor of heat.
5. The box had depressions to hold cooking kettles; it was constructed of wood or some other poor conductor of heat.
6. Some fireless cookers had stone disks which could be removed and heated; then they were returned to the cooker for keeping food hot.
7. C
8. To use a fireless cooker, the cook would heat the food on a normal stove until it was heated thoroughly.
9. Foods that required long, slow, low-temperature cooking were suitable for fireless cooking; foods that required high temperatures were not suitable.
10. Foods such as cornmeal mush would be boiled on the stove for five minutes; then they were placed in the fireless cooker for five to ten hours.
11. If the fireless cooker was properly constructed, the mush would still be hot after ten hours.
12. Some homemade cookers, however, were not adequately insulated and would allow food to become cool.
13. C
14. If food began to cool, the cook was advised to return it to the fire to reheat it; however, the cook was also advised not to open the cooker to see how the food was getting along.
15. Fireless cookers have gone the way of the dinosaurs, although we still use some of the principles they were based on.
16. Our heavy cookware holds heat, conserving stove energy; our slow cookers extend cooking time to hours, using a minimum of electricity for heating; and our ovens are surrounded with insulating material, holding heat in.
17. Even though we don't ordinarily want to wait ten hours for our cereal to be cooked, with a fireless cooker we could start it the night before and have it ready when we get out of bed.
18. The fireless cooker would have advantages for the cook who works away from home: brown the roast before going to work, pop it into the fireless cooker, and have dinner ready on arriving home.

Exercise 29-2, p. 455. Commas and semicolons: Editing text

Added punctuation is underlined.

The Aztec Indians inhabited the area around Mexico City from approximately 1200 until 1521, when they were conquered by Hernando Cortes. One of the most civilized groups of American Indians, they lived in and around their capital city, Temochtitlan, which was located at the site of the present Mexico City.

Families lived in simple adobe houses with thatched roofs. Some of their common foods were flat corn cakes, which they called *tortillas;* a drink called *chocolate,* which they made out of cacao beans; and corn, beans, tomatoes, and chili. The men dressed in breechcloths, capes, and sandals; the women wore skirts and sleeveless blouses.

Religion was central to the life of the Aztecs. They had many gods, most of which they appeased with human sacrifices. As a consequence, warfare was conducted largely for the purpose of taking prisoners, who became objects of sacrifice. During the sacrificial rite the priests would often cut out the victim's heart with a knife made of obsidian. The Aztecs believed that human sacrifices were necessary to keep the sun rising every morning and to have success with the crops and warfare.

The Aztecs educated their children in history, religious observances, crafts, and Aztec traditions. Outstanding boys and girls were trained in special schools so that someday they could perform religious duties.

Descendants of the Aztecs still live in the area around Mexico City, still speaking their ancient language but practicing Spanish customs and religion.

CHAPTER 30

The Apostrophe

Exercise 30-1, p. 461. Apostrophes for possessive case: Changing words

1. desks'
2. James's
3. everyone's
4. Ed Knox's
5. the Mileses'
6. fox's
7. community's
8. their, theirs
9. women's
10. no one else's
11. whose
12. St. Louis's
13. father-in-law's
14. Terre Haute's
15. sheep's
16. your, yours
17. the Bahamas'
18. committee member's
19. oxen's
20. *Denver Post*'s

Exercise 30-2, p. 463. Apostrophes for contractions and plurals

A.

1. doesn't
35. they're
36. it's
37. who's
38. let's
39. they've
40. I've

B.

1. M.A.'s (or MAs)
2. Ph.D.'s
3. MBAs
4. 6s or 6's
5. qts.
6. *of*s or *of*'s

Exercise 30-3, p. 458. Apostrophes: Editing text

Changes are underlined.

In my job delivering pizzas, I have learned a lot more about the city than I knew before. I have driven to many unfamiliar neighborhoods and have come to know many new people. I've also been lost many times, trying to find a house or an apartment or trying to read its address in the dark—all, of course, while the pizzas grew cold.

My first week's experience was one of the worst. I was delivering a large pepperoni supreme to the Swansons on 49th Street SE. I drove right out to 49th Street but couldn't find the Swansons' address. I found out the hard way that 49th Street stops at the river and that 49th Street SE starts somewhere on the other side of the river, with no bridge connecting the two sections. Once I found the right section of the street, I drove to the house with no problem. Their name was on a board out in front: THE SWANSONS, it said. "It's cold," they told me when they took the pizza, but they didn't complain. They said they would warm it in their microwave oven.

Another time I had to deliver fifteen pizzas to a large party on the north side of the city. I found the place without any trouble, and the pizzas were still hot when I got there, but the people who ordered couldn't decide who was going to pay me. The guy said the responsibility was hers because she had decided what kind to get and ordered them. But she said, "No, it's his place to pay for them." It seems that she didn't have enough money to pay for fifteen pizzas. They finally agreed to split the cost. That made me feel a lot better; I was getting worried about what to say to my boss when I brought all those pizzas back.

Now that I know the city well, I'll probably have to quit my job because it's taking too much of my time while I'm in school. At first I thought I would be able to reduce my hours, but my boss doesn't want to hire two people to do the job of one. I wonder where I can find another job that will use the experience I've gained from my pizza delivering but won't take too much time away from studying for my heavy load of classes.

CHAPTER 31

Quotation Marks

Exercise 31-1, p. 473. Quotation marks: Editing sentences

1. Did Cohan write "You're a Grand Old Flag"?
2. C
3. Did I hear you say, "The show is sold out"?
4. The committee declared, "'America' would be a more appropriate national anthem than the 'Star-Spangled Banner' is."
5. "Never take Route 1 unless you like traffic jams," he stated.
6. "African man," writes Mbiti, "lives in a religious universe."
7. Dickinson's poem first sets the mood: "A quietness distilled, / As twilight long begun."
8. Truman states, "I fired General MacArthur because he would not respect the authority of the President."
9. "Remember the Alamo!" was first used as a battle cry at San Jacinto.
10. "Dandruff" is the code name that CB operators give to snow.
11. Coleridge was ridiculed for writing "I hail thee brother" in his poem "To a Young Ass."
12. "The Congo" is a poem that experiments with rhythmic effects.
13. "Why did you shout 'Eureka!' as you left?" she asked.
14. We spent a whole class discussing the word "moral," yet we never agreed on its meaning.
15. The characters in the story are, in the author's words, "anti-heroes"; however, none is realistic.
16. Her article, "The Joy of Anguish," was reprinted in six languages.
17. "Sotweed" is a synonym for "tobacco."
18. "How many of you know the 'To be or not to be' speech from *Hamlet*?" asked the drama coach.
19. C
20. William Blake's poem "The Fly" includes this stanza:

    Am not I
    A fly like thee?
    Or art not thou
    A man like me?

Exercise 31-2, p. 475 Quotations: Rewriting text

Sample answers:

A. Cooling Off

When I was twelve, I went swimming at St. Ben's College swimming pool with my good friend Paul, who is two years older than I. It was a steamy hot summer day when I suggested to Paul, "Let's go for a dip."

Chuckling, he told me, "You've read my mind."

We left in the early afternoon, cruising down the road on our mud-covered bicycles. As we got to the pool, Paul yelled, "The last one in is the biggest loser in the world." Naturally he won, because I had to lock up the bikes.

Two walls of the indoor pool were enclosed in glass, affording a view of the entire campus and the sunny summer day. After we had been swimming for about an hour, I noticed that the sun was no longer shining. In fact, the sky was turning quite dark. I pointed to the leaden gray clouds moving toward us and asked Paul, "Do you think we should leave?"

He exclaimed, "Yes—after one more dive."

As we dressed in the locker room, I told Paul, "I'm nervous about the weather, because I've never seen it change so quickly." When we pushed open the door, the wind pushed back. Rushing out, we ran toward our bikes, unlocked them, and headed in the direction of home.

About halfway home, we began to be hit by small pellets of hail. Paul yelled at me, "Hurry up; you're falling behind!" With lightning brightening the dark afternoon, thunder crashing around us, and hail bouncing off our chilled bodies, we pedaled furiously, seeing my driveway just ahead. As I turned in to the drive, Paul rode on to his house next door, yelling to me, "I'll see you later!"

I dropped my bike on the lawn and dashed into the house, looking for a towel and some dry, warm clothes. I wasn't hot any more.

B. Spoiled Brats?

There is speculation that the People's Republic of China may become a nation of spoiled brats. In an article already several years old, *Time* magazine (7 Dec. 1987) estimates, "There may be hundreds of thousands, perhaps millions, of children throwing tantrums throughout China" (38). That is because of a law that China began enforcing in 1979 decreeing, "Each couple should have only one child." *Time* suggests, "These children, called 'little emperors' by the local press, have been swaddled in the love of their parents and grandparents, and as a result they are growing up spoiled, selfish, and lazy" (38).

The *China Daily* provides an example of one of these little empresses. The article states, "The girl's mother combs the little girl's hair, her grandmother feeds her breakfast, her grandfather is under the table putting her shoes on, and her father is getting her satchel ready" *(Time* 38). *Time* quotes one little girl, who said, "I ride on my Daddy's shoulders and ask my parents to make a circle with their arms. Then I say to them, 'You are the sky, and I am the little red sun'" (38).

The Chinese government is somewhat concerned about the long-term effects of the one-child-per-couple policy. When 21,000 children were asked to write a short paper on what they wanted to be when they grew up, only 5 percent said, "We want to be workers." *Time* reports, "Most wanted to become taxi drivers, hotel attendants, or Premier, because those occupations are perceived to be easy and comfortable" (38). In a communist country dependent upon workers, such an attitude is serious indeed.

Just as serious is the fear for the time when these pampered children grow up and their parents grow old. *Time* suggests, "The new generation will be unwilling to care for aging parents and geriatric grandparents, forcing the elderly into the care of the state" (38).

To deal with the situation, the Chinese government is conducting parenting courses throughout the country. New parents are told, "Don't give in to blackmail. Let the child cry all night; by the next day everything will be forgotten" (38).

But perhaps the situation is exaggerated. One Chinese psychologist says, "Single children seem to fare better than those with siblings in terms of intellectual development, and some children with siblings are even worse brats than those without them" (38). Some Chinese say, "What is important is moral education at home, whether the family has one child or many" (38).

CHAPTER 32

Other Punctuation Marks

Exercise 32-1, p. 483. The colon, the dash, parentheses, brackets, the ellipsis mark, and the slash: Editing sentences

Sample answers:

1. one—New England—had
2 reasonably ($200).
3. "spondee"—all
4. either/or
5. (1) the zone and (2) the man to man.
6. quality: tact.
7. savings—$$100—are
8. recipe (my aunt's favorite) calls
9. insignificant—only
10. Hughy) are
11. C
12. poopsite [*sic*]
13. course: Elementary
14. kit items: a
15. Hemingway (1899-1961) was
16. title (associate fireman) brought
17. hide (alligator) could
18. one: pages
19. 1295 (?), was
20. fountain"—that
21. and . . . how
22. C
23. *Works* (volumes 2 and 3) was
24. assignment: the
25. teacher (actually, his assistant) wrote

Exercise 32-2, p. 485. Punctuation: Review of Chapters 27-32

Added punctuation is underlined.

A. Threat to the Eyes

Sunlight is made up of three kinds of radiation: (1) infrared rays, which we cannot see: (2) visible rays, and (3) ultraviolet rays, which also are invisible. Especially in the ultraviolet range, sunlight is harmful to the eyes. Ultraviolet rays can damage the retina, the area in the back of the eye, and cause cataracts on the lens. Wavelengths of light rays are measured in nanometers (nm), or millionths of a meter. Infrared rays are the longest, measuring 700 nm and longer, and ultraviolet rays are the shortest, measuring 400 nm and shorter. The lens absorbs much of the ultraviolet radiation, thus protecting the retina; however, in so doing, it becomes a victim, growing cloudy and blocking vision.

You can protect your eyes by wearing sunglasses that screen out the ultraviolet rays. To be effective, sunglasses should block out at least 95 percent of the radiation. Many lenses have been designed to do exactly this, but many others are extremely ineffective. When you are buying sunglasses, you can test their effectiveness by putting them on and looking in a mirror while you stand in a bright light. If you can see your eyes through the lenses, the glasses will not screen out enough ultraviolet light to protect your eyes.

People who spend very much time outside in the sun really owe it to themselves to buy a pair of sunglasses that will shield their eyes.

B. Paradise Next Door

Belize, a small country on the eastern coast of Central America, covers less than 9000 square miles. Bordering Mexico on the north and Guatemala on the west and south, this little nation has a population of approximately 154,000. The official language is English, but Spanish and native Creole dialects are spoken as well. The country, which was formerly known as British Honduras, achieved independence in 1981. Home to Mayan Indians for centuries, Belize was settled in the seventeenth century by pirates, slavers, and shipwrecked British seamen and was ruled by Great Britain until its independence. It still maintains strong ties to the United Kingdom.

While sugar is its primary export, Belize is known mainly for diving, fishing, and swimming. Divers come from all over the world to explore its coral reefs and limestone caves. The reef offshore is 176 miles long, exceeded in length only by Australia's Great Barrier Reef. Divers also like to explore the Blue Hole, a chasm in the Caribbean that is 400 feet deep and 1000 feet wide. It has stalactites and beautiful corals.

Both the reef and the Blue Hole can be reached by boat from Belize City. This city, once the capital of the country, is now a tourist attraction because of its location. Belize City is still the largest city in Belize, but it has been replaced as capital by Belmopan, which is located fifty miles inland. In this new location, the government buildings are more secure from hurricanes.

The tallest structure in the country is the ruins called El Castillo, built about 1500 years ago by Mayan Indians. Other Mayan ruins are tucked within thick jungles and give spectacular evidence of the ancient civilization.

A major aspect of the Belize economy is the tourist trade; however, investors and developers have been attracted to the country too. Its stable government and tropical climate, both of which spur tourism, have drawn foreign business as well. Only two hours by plane from New Orleans or Houston, Belize is a near neighbor that approximates the romance of faraway places.

VIII MECHANICS

CHAPTER 33

Capitals

Exercise 33-1, p. 493. Capitals: Rewriting sentences

No sample answers.

CHAPTER 34

Underlining or Italics

Exercise 34-1, p. 499. Underlining or italics: Editing sentences

1. The cast received a standing ovation for its performance of August Wilson's <u>Fences</u>.
2. C
3. <u>The Washington Star</u> usually printed conservative views.
4. C
5. We took a tour of a ship, the <u>North Carolina</u>, for only $2.50.
6. <u>Hamlet</u> contains more violence than does any crime drama on television.
7. When I averaged all my <u>A</u>'s and <u>B</u>'s, I found that my final grade would be a <u>B</u>.
8. <u>Life</u> magazine is a showcase for photography.
9. Shaw's <u>Man and Superman</u> is more often read than viewed on stage.
10. The Great Wall of China was completed in the third century BC.

11. The strange form was the mem of the Hebrew alphabet.

12. She makes the dots on her i's so large that the page looks like an aerial view of the Charles County Balloon Festival.

13. C

14. We had to report on the P.W. Joyce book Old Celtic Romances.

15. Gree is an archaic word meaning "satisfaction."

16. A new journal, Fun with Caries, reprinted an article by Brady Hull, DDS.

17. The documentary program 60 Minutes continues to be quite profitable for CBS.

18. Miserere is the fifty-first psalm in the Douay Bible.

19. The expression c'est la vie never gave me much comfort.

20. The professor published her article in the sociology journal Studies in Poverty.

21. I was surprised to see that Wyeth's Christina's World is not a larger painting.

22. The foxglove belongs to the genus Digitalis.

23. My husband repeatedly mispronounces the word asterisk.

24. My twenty-year subscription to Boys' Life, given to me by my uncle, has finally expired.

CHAPTER 35

Abbreviations

Exercise 35-1, p. 505. Abbreviations: Editing sentences

1. Jan.—January
2. Econ.—Economics
3. Tues.—Tuesday; Ch.—Chapter
4. Wm.—William; Dec.—December
5. C
6. U.—University
7. e.g.—for example
8. assoc. prof.—associate professor
9. C *or* U.S. Congress
10. C *or* Saint Paul
11. Tex.—Texas; Off.—Office
12. WY—Wyoming
13. etc.—and so forth
14. N.Y.—New York
15. CA—California
16. no.—number
17. C
18. Ms—Ms.

CHAPTER 36

Numbers

Exercise 36-1, p. 509. Numbers: Editing sentences

1. C
2. ~~June 1st~~ —June 1
3. C
4. ~~two thousand~~ —2000
5. ~~500~~ —five hundred
6. ~~Eighteen~~ —18
7. ~~seven percent~~ —7 percent
8. ~~7,800~~ —seven thousand eight hundred
9. ~~9~~ —nine
10. C
11. C
12. ~~December 29 th~~ —December 29
13. C *or* fifteen dollars
14. C
15. ~~1 troy ounce~~ —One troy ounce
16. C
17. ~~12 th~~ —twelfth
18. C

CHAPTER 37

Word Division

Exercise 37-1, p. 513. Dividing words correctly

The following words are divided according to *The American Heritage Dictionary of the English Language*, 3rd ed. (Boston: Houghton Mifflin, 1992); dictionaries differ on how to divide some words.

1. con-
   trolled
2. accom-
   plish
3. Marxist-
   Leninist
4. achieve
5. C
6. head-
   hunting
7. poetry
8. pan-
   African
9. swarthy
10. tech-
    nique
11. self-
    inflicted
12. length
13. C
14. rented
15. C

Exercise 37-2, p. 514. Dividing electronic addresses

Sample answers; other divisions following slashes are permissible:

1. http://owl.english.purdue.edu/
   Files/26.html
2. http://www.uottawa.ca/academic/
   arts/writcent
3. http://members.home.net/
   kayem/idioms/idioms.html
4. http://leo.stcloudstate.edu/style/
   wordiness.html
5. http://www.aitech.ac.jp/~iteslj/
   quizzes/idioms.html
6. http://www.esc.edu/htmlpages/
   writer/style1.htm#denot

IX EFFECTIVE WORDS

CHAPTER 38

Choosing and Using Words

Exercise 38-1, p. 527. Appropriate words: Revising text

Revisions are underlined. Sample answers:

1. When a person dies, the body undergoes specific changes. The tissues do not receive oxygen and the cells begin to degrade when they no longer have any energy supplied through ATP synthesis. Once death occurs and the brain has ceased functioning, the temperature of the body begins to drop. The amount is about one degree to one and a half degrees per hour— dependent on other factors, such as the temperature of the environment and the size of the body. An obvious change is the one called *rigor mortis*. As all mystery fans know, this is the stiffening of the body that begins one or two hours after death. The first to stiffen are the eyelids, then the rest of the face. For the next twelve hours, the rigor progresses downward until the entire body is affected. The stiffness begins to disappear and a waxy appearance begins to form after about thirty-six hours.

2. Political candidates have discovered that women make up over half of the eligible voting population. The trouble is that many women are thinking so much about their own concerns that they are not totally aware of what the issues are—or what these candidates think they are. Women with young children get more involved with getting their children off to school with both shoes on than they do in themselves and which candidate promises them the most or looks the best on television. So the competitors attempt to learn just how to get possession of the votes of this constituency.

Exercise 38-2, p. 529. Biased language: Revising sentences

Revisions are underlined. Sample answers:

1. Pastor and Mrs. Olsen will be honored guests at the luncheon. (*Or* Pastor and Barbara Olsen)
2. Students should have their books by the first day of class.
3. The mail carrier was half an hour late today.
4. Under normal circumstances, wolves do not attack people.
5. Employees should fill out their time cards before the end of the day.
6. That elderly man driving down the road looks as if he can hardly see over the steering wheel.
7. If you have any trouble with the washing machine, just call your service technician.
8. I was stopped at a traffic light when a woman driving a Suburban rammed the rear of my car.

9. Nurses are always expected to put duty before personal interests.
10. Has everybody put his or her name at the top of the paper? *or* Have you all put your names at the top of your papers?
11. Every police officer in this city is equipped with a bullet-proof vest.
12. Check the wind forecast before going out in a boat. *Or* People who want to fish should check the wind forecast before going out in a boat.
13. The divers went deeper than anyone has ever gone before.
14. The man is probably a member of AARP and writes his Congressperson every week.
15. "Madam chair," he said, "I'd like five minutes for answering the question."
16. We took the broken toy to the woman at the service desk.
17. My uncle wanted to know if I had met any attractive women yet on campus.
18. Doctors have to hire someone to keep up on their paper work for Medicare.
19. Anyone who wants to reserve a room has to use a credit card.
20. The religious fundamentalists in the building down the street were practicing speaking in tongues.
21. The old man was helping his elderly wife up the steps so they could go in and vote.
22. It seemed as if all the pharmacists at the convention were signing their names on the suppliers' lists.
23. Writers must always consider their readers.
24. Sylvia wondered if the tiger in the cage ate humans in its natural state.

Exercise 38-3, p. 531. Denotation: Comparing forms

1. accept
2. affected
3. every day
4. compliment
5. implied
6. allusions
7. irritated
8. number
9. sometime
10. may be
11. than
12. already
13. likely
14. eager
15. conscious
16. fewer
17. idea
18. proceeded

Exercise 38-4, p. 532. General and specific words, abstract and concrete words: revising text

Sample answers:

1. My 9:00 a.m. class in World War II history did not meet today because Professor Jackson had to attend a curriculum meeting. So I spent the hour in the cafeteria, eating a cream-cheese bagel, drinking cafe au lait and studying for my calculus exam.

2. The candidate for sheriff announced to the townspeople that he would support two-parent families, the right to bear arms, and capital punishment. He would bring observance for the law to the position and would carry out its duties with the hope of reward.

3. My favorite place in all the world is my family's cabin on Green Lake. Last summer my friend Linda and I spent five days there, and they were relaxing and exciting at the same time. We got up about ten o'clock in the morning, went for a walk in the oak and pine woods, and then after having a lunch cooked in the rugged cabin we'd stretch out on a granite rock about ten by twenty feet across and snooze for a while before taking a dip in the crystal clear water. Afternoons we'd go

out in the family's rowboat. Maybe we'd fish and maybe just row around the shoreline. One day we caught a seven-pound walleye, so we broiled it over the open coals for supper. Boy, did it taste sweet and juicy.

4. The sunflowers on the serving table in the banquet hall had begun to wilt as a result of the 90-degree heat and a lack of water. The matronly hostess tried to revive them by pouring a cupful of water into the porcelain vase and spritzing them with a bottle of lavender-scented water.

Exercise 38-5, p. 533. Idioms: Comparing forms

1.	for	8.	with
2.	with	9.	for
3.	with	10.	of
4.	for	11.	in
5.	with	12.	with
6.	from	13.	with
7.	of	14.	for

Exercise 38-6, p. 534. Trite expressions: Revising sentences

Sample answers:

1. He writes well, but he is not an immortal artist.
2. Balancing our budget is a reasonable approach to take.
3. Showing great potential, my little brother won a mathematics award and two science awards.
4. We could wait forever to see a solution to hostilities in the Middle East.
5. Moving my grandfather to a nursing home was more difficult than we expected.
6. I did not know for sure, but I suspected that my friends were planning a surprise party.
7. I understand your message.
8. The sight of my old rival startled me.
9. We may have to make some sacrifices before we see an end to the budget crisis.
10. I was shocked when I saw the utility bill.

Exercise 38-7, p. 535. Empty words and phrases: Revising text

Sample answers:

People who live in the "Frost Belt," ~~otherwise known as the northern states~~, are, ~~at this point in time~~, still moving toward the sun. According to the 1990 census, cities ~~situated~~ in the northern part of the United States decreased in size while cities ~~located~~ in the South increased. New York City, for example, decreased ~~and diminished~~ by 38,460 residents, Detroit ~~decreased~~ by 233,213, and Chicago ~~decreased~~ by 279,093. ~~As a matter of fact,~~ only two ~~of the big and~~ major cities in the

Northeast and Midwest did not lose residents: Columbus, Ohio, and Indianapolis, Indiana. In contrast, every big city ~~that is~~ located ~~in the areas~~ of the South and Southwest—with two exceptions—gained residents. The two exceptions ~~that were noted~~ are Memphis and New Orleans.

According to the new figures, New York City is still~~, at the present time,~~ the largest city in the nation, but Los Angeles~~, a city situated in the area of the South,~~ takes the place of Chicago~~, which is a city located in the northern area,~~ as the second largest, and Houston, another southern city, replaced Philadelphia~~, a northern city,~~ as fourth largest. Detroit moved down from sixth place to ninth, and San Antonio achieved the top ten.

~~The point is that~~ cities affected by changes ~~and alterations~~ in population experience ~~serious and~~ dire consequences because ~~due to the fact that~~ the census counted fewer people. The ~~first and~~ foremost consequence ~~that exists~~ is a decrease in federal funding~~, for the reason that it is~~ based on population. Another is decreased political clout because ~~, due to the fact that~~ representation, like funding, is based on numbers of residents.

~~It seems that~~ in 2000 some cities and the Census Bureau attempted ~~to get~~ a more accurate census count. These cities charged that in 1990 many residents—thousands or even millions—were not counted. New York City, for example, charged that a million of its people were not counted, a loss of $1.5 billion for the city ~~for a period extending~~ throughout the 1990s. City officials said that among those not counted were minorities, homeless people, and illegal immigrants. ~~For all intents and purposes,~~ these are all people that cities provide services for but have not received federal funding under the 1990 count.

But even with a more accurate count~~, and all things considered,~~ the census still revealed a steady population trend toward ~~the region of~~ the South.

CHAPTER 39

Using Dictionaries

Exercise 39-1, p. 539. Using the dictionary

The answers given here are drawn from The American Heritage Dictionary, 2nd college ed. Other dictionaries might provide different information in a different form.

A. Abbreviations

- a. synonym (abbreviation not used)
- b. dialectal
- c. pronoun
- d. Greek
- e. obsolete
- f. intransitive verb

B. Spelling

- a. speak·eas·y
- b. back·wa·ter
- c. liv·ing room
- d. cat·like
- e. hay·loft
- f. freeze·dry
- g. It·a·ly
- h. self·gov·ern·ment

C. Pronunciation

- a. păs'tər·əl
- b. ûr, ĕr
- c. ĭn'və·lid, in·văl'id
- d. sĭz'əm, skĭz'əm
- e. ô'fən, ŏf'ən
- f. kăr·ə·bē'ən, kə'rĭb'e·ən
- g. kĭln, kĭl
- h. ĭ·rĕl'·ə·vənt

D. Grammatical functions and forms

1. a. *preferred* (past tense and past participle)
   b. *worked* (past tense and past participle)
   c. *broke* (past tense), *broken* (past participle)
   d. *echoed* (past tense and past participle)
   e. *wrung* (past tense and past participle)
   f. *saw* (past tense), *seen* (past participle)
2. a. no comparative and superlative forms given
   b. *lovelier, loveliest*
   c. no comparative and superlative forms given
   d. *worse, worst*
   e. no comparative and superlative forms given

E. Etymology

1.
   a.
      (1) Latin inducere
      (2) to bring in
      (3) Middle English
   b.
      (1) Latin *tenere*
      (2) to hold
      (3) Old French, Middle English
   c.
      (1) Old English *scyrte*
      (2) no meaning given
      (3) Middle English
   d.
      (1) Greek *rhuthmos*
      (2) no meaning given
      (3) Latin, Old French
2.
   a. from *zip*
   b. *jargoun,* Old French *jargon* (probably imitative)
   c. *astro* + Greek *nautes,* sailor
   d. origin unknown
   e. After Vidkun Quisling (1887-1945)

F. Meanings

a.
   (1) *biology,* category of taxonomic classification
   (2) *logic,* class of individuals or objects grouped by common attributes
b.
   (1) liver bile
   (2) rancor; bitterness
c.
   (1) to pursue relentlessly
   (2) to urge insistently
d.
   (1) to move along; proceed
   (2) to move or function properly

G. Labels

a. regional (used in several areas of the United States but not nationwide)
b. informal (acceptable in conversation but not in formal writing)
c. slang (transitory expression intended to produce an effect)

H. Other information

1. In a separate section beginning on p. 1409.
2. In a separate section beginning on p. 1466.
3. No
4. Yes
5. Yes

CHAPTER 40

Improving Your Vocabulary

Exercise 40-1, p. 549. Roots, prefixes, suffixes: Inferred meanings

Answers in this chapter are based on The American Heritage Dictionary, 2nd college ed.

1. adj., pertaining to or engaged in warfare
2. adj., placed in front
3. v., to divide or distribute proportionately
4. adj., applying to a period prior to enactment
5. v., to speak in favor of; n., person who argues for a cause
6. n., admirer of France and its people and customs (also adj.)
7. v., to prohibit or place under ecclesiastical or legal sanction (also n.)
8. n., chemical compound consisting of many repeated linked units
9. v., to undermine
10. n., radio receiver and transmitter, used for sending and receiving signals across space
11. n., 1000 cycles
12. v., to scatter or distribute among other things at irregular intervals
13. n., leader of the common people
14. adj., lacking moral distinctions or judgments
15. v., to rise above or across

Exercise 40-2, p. 550. Contextual Clues: Inferred Meanings

Sample answers:

1.	demographic:	pertaining to populations, including age
	imperative:	something necessary, mandatory
2.	disaffection:	opposite of liking; lost affection or loyalty
	draconian:	harsh, severe
3.	latitude:	freedom from limitations
	sophisticated:	unusual; complex
	surveillance:	means of investigation; close observation
4.	skeptical:	doubting; questioning
	putative:	supposed; doubtful

CHAPTER 41

Spelling and the Hyphen

Exercise 41-1, p. 563. Commonly confused words

1. effect, one's
2. passed, its
3. personal, stationery
4. It's, who's
5. poor, role
6. led
7. cite, site, their
8. affect, your
9. affects
10. led, bearing
11. whose, your
12. which, led
13. principal
14. reign, to
15. descent, which

Exercise 41-2, p. 565. Spelling rules: Practice

A.

1. achieve
2. weight
3. friend
4. chief
5. sleigh
6. height
7. receive
8. neither
9. believe
10. hygiene
11. forfeit
12. conceit
13. seize
14. deceit

B.

1. noticing, noticeable
2. hating, hateful
3. surely, surest
4. agreeing, agreeable
5. dutiful, duties
6. truest, truly
7. defying, defiance
8. studying, studied

C.

1. difference
2. traveled
3. submitted
4. referred
5. occurrence
6. permitted
7. beginning
8. stopping
9. preference
10. preferring
11. shipment
12. begging

D.	1.	buffaloes	7.	series
	2.	tomatoes	8.	indexes
	3.	mothers-in-law	9.	handfuls
	4.	sheep	10.	passersby
	5.	shelves	11.	analyses
	6.	foxes	12.	economies

Exercise 41-3, p. 567. The hyphen in compound words, fractions, and compound numbers: Practice

A.
1. ten and one-quarter
2. twenty-one twenty-seconds
3. thirty-nine
4. one hundred two
5. three million one hundred fifty-two
6. ninety-two
7. twenty-five
8. twenty-five thousand ninety-five
9. three-tenths
10. two hundred sixty

B.	1.	ante-bellum *or* antebellum	4.	carport
			5.	porch light
	2.	pro-American	6.	newsstand
	3.	self-serving	7.	hot dog *or* hotdog
	8.	nonpartisan	15.	red-handed
	9.	ninth-century warfare	16.	softhearted
	10.	co-author *or* coauthor	17.	prefabricated
	11.	post-Victorian	18.	lifeboat
	12.	redeyed *or* red-eyed rabbit	19.	lifelike
	13.	reshuffle	20.	anti-imperialist
	14.	long-handled		

X WORKING WITH SOURCES

CHAPTER 42

Writing a Short Documented Paper

Exercise 42-1, p. 583. Writing paraphrases

Sample answers:

1. Referring to the work of Galileo, Stephen W. Hawking says that the Renaissance astronomer believed the Copernican theory of planets orbiting the sun long before he spoke of it publicly, keeping it to himself until he had sufficient evidence to support it (A Brief History of Time 179).

2. Evidence now reveals that the illness that struck President Woodrow Wilson in April 1919 was not influenza as diagnosed by his doctor but, instead, a thrombosis of the brain. The faulty diagnosis is not surprising, however, considering the global proportions of the flu epidemic at that time (Smith 101).

3. In Freedom and Beyond, John Holt criticizes bureaucracies as organizations so locked into past experience that they cannot learn from the present (45).

4. Political education, says Henry Adams, must be adapted to the locale where it is being practiced. Learning about human nature in Westminster, England, for example, is of no use politically in Paris or America (198).

5. According to Jean Strause in Up Against the Law, social pressure brings about changes in the law. New laws are made, she says, not to introduce social change but to respond to public awareness of a need for change. When they are passed, they legitimize rights that the public has already debated (20).

Exercise 42-2, p. 585. Identifying plagiarism

Revisions are sample answers.

1. Plagiarized words: When the Roman empire was at its zenith; the passionate Mystery religions; provided . . . community spirit
   Revision: At the peak of the Roman empire, the Mystery religions gave people a cohesion and community spirit that might not otherwise have been available (Grant 185).

2. Plagiarized words: moral perfectibility; (no citation)
Revision: According to Michael Grant, Stoics were concerned mainly with ethics and "moral perfectibility" (218).

3. OK

4. Plagiarized words: almost mind; (inadequate citation)
Revision: Tuchman remarks that no one knows what Asquith's "almost mind" thought about this question (72).

5. Plagiarized words: mysterious distribution of animals and plants; changing continent shapes; changing flow of ocean currents; (no citation)
Revision: Paleontologists attribute the otherwise unexplainable distribution of many plants and animals to alterations in continent shapes and changes in ocean currents (Carson 30).

Exercise 42-3, p. 587. Writing bibliographic entries

1. **4** Frank, Francine Wattman, and Paula A. Treichler. Language, Gender, and Professional Writing: Theoretical Approaches and Guidelines for Nonsexist Usage. New York: MLA, 1989.
2. **8** Rieff, David. "Zagreb Dispatch: Go West Young Country." New Republic 17 January 2000: 15-17.
3. **10** "Tactical Recommendations." <http://www.sonoma.edu/tsrecom.nclk> (5 March 2000)
4. **6** Geertz, Clifford. Local Knowledge: Further Essays in Interpretive Anthropology. New York: Basic, 1983.
5. **7** Geok-lin, Shirley, Mayumi Tsutakawa, and Margarita Donnelly, eds. The Forbidden Stitch: An Asian American Women's Anthology. Corvallis: Calyx, 1989.
6. **3** Denault, Leigh. "19th Century Women's Literature." Rivendell's American Literature Page. <http://fledge.watson.org/rivendell/chopin%26gilman.html> (14 January 2000). [Electronic addresses may be divided after a slash.]
7. **9** Sharpe, Patricia, Frances Mascia-Lees, and Colleen B. Cohen. "White Women and Black Men: Differential Responses to Reading Black Women's Texts." College English 52 (1990): 142-53.
8. **11** Taylor, B. L. "Conservation Update." Burlington Times 2 February 1996: B3. Rpt. online. Expanded Academic Index (4 February 1999). [The first date is date of publication, the second date of viewing.]
9. **1** "Associate Degree Standards." <http://www.heso.state.mn.us/www/privinst/assocdeg.htm.> (27 February 1999).
10. **2** Bures, Frank. "Stingy Is Best When Using Skin Medicine." St. Cloud (Minn.) Times 12 August 1990: C4.
11. **5** Fritts, Steven H. "Wolves." New Grolier Multimedia Encyclopedia. CD-ROM. 1993.
12. **12** Tenson, Carl. "Hypertext Today." MUD History. Online. Internet. <http://www.nnt.cos.edu/mud-history.html> (3 March 1999).